CAMPAIGN • 240

WABASH 1791

St Clair's defeat

JOHN F WINKLER

ILLUSTRATED BY PETER DENNIS

Series editor Marcus Cowper

First published in Great Britain in 2011 by Osprey Publishing,
Midland House, West Way, Botley, Oxford, OX2 0PH, UK
44-02 23rd Street, Suite 219, Long Island City, NY 11101, USA

E-mail: info@ospreypublishing.com

Osprey Publishing is part of the Osprey Group.

A CIP catalog record for this book is available from the British Library.

Print ISBN: 978 1 84908 676 9
PDF e-book ISBN: 978 1 84908 677 6
EPUB e-book ISBN: 978 1 84908 893 0

Editorial by Ilios Publishing Ltd, Oxford, UK (www.iliospublishing.com)
Design: The Black Spot
Index by Alison Worthington
Originated by Blenheim Colour
Cartography: Boundford.com
Bird's-eye view artworks: The Black Spot
Printed in China through Worldprint, China

11 12 13 14 15   10 9 8 7 6 5 4 3 2 1

www.ospreypublishing.com

ACKNOWLEDGMENTS

Nancy Meiring Knapke and Christine Keller of the Fort Recovery State
Museum offered invaluable advice and assistance in assembling the materials
for this book. Judy Bratten, Sonja Cropper, Robert Hart, Phyllis Helphenstine,
Joan Kearns, Brianna Parrish, Jonathan Reed Winkler, and Wendy King Winkler
generously provided their help in taking or finding site photographs.

ARTIST'S NOTE

Readers may care to note that the original paintings from which the
color plates in this book were prepared are available for private sale.
The Publishers retain all reproduction copyright whatsoever.
All enquiries should be addressed to:

Peter Dennis, Fieldhead, The Park, Mansfield, Notts, NG18 2AT

The Publishers regret that they can enter into no correspondence upon
this matter.

THE WOODLAND TRUST

Osprey Publishing are supporting the Woodland Trust, the UK's leading
woodland conservation charity, by funding the dedication of trees.

MEASUREMENT CONVERSIONS

Imperial measurements are used almost exclusively throughout this book.
The exception is weapon calibers, which are given in their official
designation, whether metric or imperial. The following data will
help in converting the imperial measurements to metric.

1 mile = 1.6km
1lb = 0.45kg
1oz = 28g
1 yard = 0.9m
1ft = 0.3m
1in. = 2.54cm/25.4mm
1 gal = 4.5 liters
1pt = 0.47 liters
1 ton (US) = 0.9 tonnes
1hp = 0.745kW

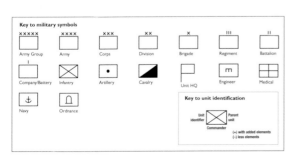

CONTENTS

INTRODUCTION   5

THE STRATEGIC SITUATION   6
The Ohio River frontier . The Northwest Territory . Harmar's campaign

CHRONOLOGY   16

OPPOSING COMMANDERS   18
American . Indian

OPPOSING ARMIES   23
American . Indian . Orders of battle

OPPOSING PLANS   31
American . Indian

THE CAMPAIGN AND BATTLE   38
The American advance . The battle of the Wabash . The American retreat

AFTERMATH   88

THE BATTLEFIELD TODAY   92

BIBLIOGRAPHY   94

INDEX   95

The situation in eastern North America in 1791

British Quebec

Lake Superior

Quebec

Montreal

St Lawrence River

MASSACHUSETTS

DISPUTED BRITISH AND AMERICAN

Fort Mackinac

Lake Huron

VERMONT

NEW HAMPSHIRE

Lake Michigan

Lake Ontario

Fort Niagara

NEW YORK

MASSACHUSETTS

Boston

Fort Detroit

Lake Erie

Allegheny River

CONNECTICUT

RHODE ISLAND

NORTHWEST TERRITORY OF THE UNITED STATES

Fort Franklin

PENNSYLVANIA

New York

Fort Mcintosh

Fort Pitt

Wabash River

OHIO COUNTRY

Philadelphia

NEW JERSEY

Fort Washington

Fort Harmar

MARYLAND

DELAWARE

St Louis

Post Vincennes

Fort Steuben

Ohio River

Alexandria

SPANISH LOUISIANA

KENTUCKY

VIRGINIA

Richmond

SOUTHWEST TERRITORY OF THE UNITED STATES

Holston River

Kingsport

NORTH CAROLINA

Mississippi River

Tennessee River

SOUTH CAROLINA

GEORGIA

Charleston

ATLANTIC OCEAN

Savannah

SPANISH WEST FLORIDA

New Orleans

St Augustine

GULF OF MEXICO

SPANISH EAST FLORIDA

N

■ US Army fort
□ British fort
● City or town
░ British territory
░ Spanish territory
░ Independent territory
░ Disputed territory
░ US national territory
░ US state territory

0   200 miles

0   200km

INTRODUCTION

In 1791, the federal government of the United States faced its first crisis. Two years into the presidency of George Washington and four years after ratification of the US Constitution, raids by American Indians living in what is now Ohio had become intolerable. Unless the United States acted to take control of the area between the Ohio River and the Great Lakes, the new nation would have no future west of the Appalachian Mountains.

The federal government's 300-man US Army was too small to undertake a campaign against the Ohio Indians. To create a sufficient force, the government recruited soldiers from across the United States. To lead them in a difficult mission on the remote Ohio River frontier, Washington looked to men who had proven their ability to command. He summoned from retirement the Continental Army officers with whom he had won American independence at Yorktown ten years before.

Major-General Arthur St Clair, who had been one of Washington's principal lieutenants, assembled at Cincinnati about 2,000 badly trained and ill-equipped soldiers. He then led them into the dense and trackless Ohio forests. Hindered by geographical ignorance, difficult terrain, bad weather, illness, and a lack of supplies, the Americans advanced as far as the Wabash River. There, at what is now Fort Recovery, Ohio, an Indian army awaited them.

On November 4, 1791, more than 3,000 Americans and Indians met at the battle of the Wabash. Few engagements in American military history were more dramatic. Revolutionary War heroes, legendary frontiersmen, and celebrated Indian chiefs and warriors fought in the Ohio woods the greatest of all battles between Americans and Indians. Three hours of combat tested the armies' very-different tactics and weapons. Concentrated Americans faced dispersed Indians. American artillery and bayonets confronted Indian muskets, bows, and tomahawks. By the time it ended, about 800 Americans were dead, more than had fallen in any battle of the Revolutionary War, and more than would fall on any battlefield before the Civil War. Hundreds more were wounded.

THE STRATEGIC SITUATION

THE OHIO RIVER FRONTIER

In 1791 the United States had about four million citizens, most of whom lived within 100 miles of the Atlantic Ocean. The territory of the United States, however, included a vast area to the west. Beyond the Appalachian Mountains about 230,000 American settlers lived in frontier counties of Pennsylvania, frontier counties of Virginia that would become Kentucky and West Virginia, and two areas controlled by the US national government. The first federal area, usually called the Southwest Territory, would in time become the state of Tennessee. The other, the Northwest Territory, would become Ohio, Indiana, Illinois, Michigan, Wisconsin and part of Minnesota.

Americans crossed the Appalachians through a series of large valleys that divided the eastern and western ranges of the mountains. An Indian trail, improved to form the Great Wagon Road, led southwest through the valleys to what is now Kingsport, Tennessee, and the valleys of the Holston and Tennessee rivers. By 1791, about 70,000 settlers had established themselves there.

This photograph shows the Ohio River as it is now, as seen after an early winter frost, from Ripley, Ohio. (Courtesy of Brown County (Ohio) Department of Tourism)

To the northwest, beyond the western range of the Appalachians, lay the 981-mile long Ohio River, and what was generally called the Ohio Country. The Ohio Country extended west to the Wabash River, and north to Lake Erie, through what is now western Pennsylvania, West Virginia, Ohio and eastern Indiana. The area south of the Ohio River was usually called Kentucky.

Six trails through gaps in the mountains allowed American settlers to reach the Ohio River frontier. In the northeast, Forbes Road, an Indian trail improved to carry wagons, led from Carlisle, Pennsylvania, to what is now Pittsburgh. Five other trails, passable only by horses or on foot, also led to the river. That in the far southwest, known as the Wilderness Trail, extended from Kingsport to present-day Louisville.

By 1791, about 160,000 settlers lived on the Ohio River frontier, clustered in areas near the trails or along the Ohio River. Almost all lived on small farms, often many miles from their nearest neighbors. Small fortifications, usually called fort and stations, served as refuges in time of war. The largest population centers were Lexington and Washington, in the Kentucky District of Virginia, where about 500 people lived. Pittsburgh had a population of nearly 400, and Louisville of about 200.

Seven US Army forts guarded the limits of American settlement. They extended from Fort Franklin on the Allegheny River to Post Vincennes on the Wabash. Between them, forts Pitt, Mcintosh, Harmar, Washington and Steuben lay along the 705-mile-long Ohio River frontier from Pittsburgh to Louisville.

Far beyond the American forts, in what is now northwestern Ohio, northern Indiana, southern Michigan, and southern Ontario, lay territory populated by about 15,000–20,000 French, Indian, and British settlers and their descendants. A century before, the area had been unpopulated. Conflicts between the Iroquois of New York – a confederacy of the Mohawk, Oneida, Onondaga, Cayuga and Seneca tribes – and Indians as far west as the Mississippi River, had made the Ohio Country too dangerous for habitation.

When the conflicts, usually called the Beaver Wars, ended in 1701, French and Indian settlers began to repopulate the area; British settlers later joined them. By 1791, many individuals in the area were difficult to categorize as French, Indian or British. Decades of intermarriage, the adoption of captured enemies, and cultural interaction had blurred traditional identities.

By 1791 many Ohio Indians lived in log cabins rather than traditional bark-covered structures. Such cabins sometimes displayed the wealth of chiefs like Blue Jacket, who led the Shawnee at the battle. Blue Jacket, wrote the American captive Margaret Pauley, had "married a half French woman of Detroit, who lived in great style, had curtained beds and silver spoons. I was fond of visiting this house; they always seemed kind and desirous of giving me tea." The photograph is of reconstructed Schoenbrunn, a Christian Delaware village built in 1772 near New Philadelphia, Ohio. (Author's collection)

Perhaps 15,000 of the area's inhabitants were, either by traditional rules of patrilineal or matrilineal descent, or by adoption, members of the Delaware, Miami, Mingo, Ojibwe, Ottawa, Shawnee or Wyandot tribes, and of tribal subgroups. They varied, however, in the extent to which they honored tribal and subgroup loyalties and followed traditional patterns of Indian life.

More than 1,000 people lived in Detroit, the area's largest population center. There, a fort garrisoned by British regulars protected the town and nearby British and French settlers' homesteads. Near Detroit, and along the Maumee, Wabash, Auglaize and Sandusky rivers, there were many Indian villages. Around them, Indian women, children and slaves labored in fields and orchards, while Indian men hunted or warred.

In 1791 a 100-mile-wide strip of almost uninhabited land separated the American forts from the Indian villages. The strip was the result of nearly 40 years of intermittent hostilities between the Ohio Indians and the Americans. In 1755 the Ohio Indians had commenced the hostilities, in the conflict known in the United States as the French and Indian War and in Britain as the Seven Years War. Fighting as French allies, they had attacked American settlements east of the Appalachians.

In 1763, after the French had surrendered the Ohio Country to the British, the Indians resumed the attacks in Pontiac's War. In 1764 a British army led by Colonel Henry Bouquet invaded Ohio. Ten years of peace in the Ohio Country followed. During that period, American settlers began to establish themselves west of the Appalachians. In 1774 hostilities resumed in Lord Dunmore's War. At the mouth of the Kanawha River, at what is now Point Pleasant, West Virginia, a Virginia militia army defeated the Ohio Indians at the battle of Point Pleasant.

The Revolutionary War followed in 1775. The Ohio Indians, except for a pro-American faction of Delaware, fought as British allies. The British and Indians, despite many victories, were unable to drive the Americans from their forts and stations. The Americans, whose settlements in Western Pennsylvania and Kentucky were separated by hundreds of miles, were unable to coordinate their militia forces for an attack on Detroit.

Settlers in Pennsylvania and what is now West Virginia had some success on the upper Ohio River frontier. The Indians failed in their 1777 and 1782 attacks on Fort Henry, at Wheeling, West Virginia, and in a 1778 attempt to capture Fort Randolph, at Point Pleasant, West Virginia. American victories in 1781, at the battles of Coshocton, at what is now Coshocton, Ohio; Breakneck Lake, near what is now Kent, Ohio; and Salt Lick Town, at what is now Niles, Ohio, forced the Indians to abandon their villages on the Muskingum, Tuscarawas, and upper Cuyahoga rivers.

American operations on the upper Ohio River frontier were otherwise unsuccessful. In 1778 the Americans built, but could not maintain, Fort Laurens, at what is now Bolivar, Ohio. In 1782 they suffered disasters. At the Gnadenhutten Massacre a militia force embarrassed the Americans by killing 90 pacifist Christian Delaware settlers at Gnadenhutten, Ohio. At the battles of Sandusky and Olentangy, near present-day Upper Sandusky and Bucyrus, Ohio, an American invasion of Ohio ended in disaster. The Indians then destroyed the largest Pennsylvania settlement west of the Appalachians: Hannastown, near what is now Greensburg, Pennsylvania.

The Americans also suffered grave setbacks on the Kentucky front. In 1779, a militia attack on Oldtown, an Indian village near modern Xenia, Ohio, ended in large casualties. In the same year, Indians destroyed an American force at the battle of the Licking River, at what is now Newport, Kentucky. In 1780 Captain Henry Bird led a British and Indian army with artillery into Kentucky. The Indians then killed or captured almost a tenth of the Kentucky settlers when Ruddell's and Martin's stations, near modern Cynthiana, Kentucky, were forced to surrender. In 1781, at Lochry's Defeat, Indians killed or captured more than 100 American militiamen, near what is now Aurora, Indiana. In 1782, at the battle of Blue Licks, Indians killed 83 more near modern Mount Olivet, Kentucky.

Indians like Anthony Shane, who fought at the battle of Wabash as a Shawnee Warrior, had a complex genetic and cultural heritage. His Wyandot father, a prominent chief, was himself the son of a French trader who had become an adopted Ojibwe. His Shawnee mother was Tecumseh's aunt. Shane, who spoke English, French, and five Indian languages, later became a trader. He and his wife Lamateshe, a sister of the Shawnee commander Black Fish, probably lived in this cabin, which survives in Rockford, Ohio. (Author's collection)

This portrait by Raphaelle Peale depicts Brigadier-General Josiah Harmar. (Courtesy of the Diplomatic Reception Rooms, US Department of State, Washington, DC)

When led by the brilliant Colonel George Rogers Clark, however, the Kentuckians achieved important victories. Clark's daring 1779 attack on Post Vincennes, where he captured Lieutenant-Colonel Henry Hamilton and a small British force, allowed the Americans to claim the area between the Ohio River and the Great Lakes at the end the Revolutionary War. His 1780 victory at the battle of Peckuwe, near modern Springfield, Ohio, forced the Indians to retire to villages far from the Ohio River. His devastating 1782 campaign up the Miami River to avenge Blue Licks destroyed Indian villages and British trading posts as far north as Loramie's Trading Post, at modern Fort Loramie, Ohio.

In 1782, word of the great American victory at Yorktown spread in the West. News soon followed that the war would end in a treaty acknowledging American independence. Shocked, the Ohio Indians ceased large-scale operations in 1783. For a time, it appeared that war on the Ohio River frontier would end.

THE NORTHWEST TERRITORY

In 1784, Congress approved the Treaty of Paris, which ended the Revolutionary War. By then, however, it seemed unlikely that the United States would long survive. The war had left the American economy in ruins. The insolvent United States had only such funds as the member states would give it. The American states, themselves insolvent, looked for revenues from citizens who threatened rebellion whenever new taxes were proposed.

Americans had little loyalty to the United States. It existed only under the Articles of Confederation, a 1781 treaty by which the 13 member states had agreed to act in union whenever nine agreed on a course of action. The national government, which consisted of representatives of the states meeting as Congress, commanded little respect. In 1782, only intervention by George Washington had prevented officers of his army from seizing control of the national government from Congress. In 1783, only the timely arrival of loyal regiments led by Brigadier-General Josiah Harmar had saved Congress from Pennsylvania soldiers demanding promised pensions and pay.

In 1784, many believed that the Americans would ultimately separate into multiple nations. In an area claimed by both New York and New Hampshire,

This engraving from Samuel Hildreth's 1848 *Pioneer History* shows Fort Harmar, the headquarters of the US Army from 1785 until 1790. (Author's collection)

Americans had already established a state outside the United States, which they named Vermont. Areas west of the Appalachians seemed likely to produce more such states. In 1784, the "Overmountain Men" of the Holston River valley seceded from North Carolina, where Colonel John Sevier had led them to victory in 1780 at King's Mountain. Settlers in the four Pennsylvania counties west of the mountains, and in the nine counties that constituted the Kentucky District of Virginia, talked of establishing their own independent states, modeled on Sevier's new state of Frankland. Enthusiasm for a new, independent state in Kentucky soared in 1784, when Spain barred American commerce from the Mississippi River.

Many American leaders, however, recognized that permanent independence would require a common national identity, a plausible prospect of national prosperity, and a strong national government. The Treaty of Paris provided an asset they could use to achieve those goals. In it, Britain had ceded to the United States the area between the Ohio River and the Great Lakes.

Virginia, which claimed the area, offered it to the United States. There an American national government, administering American national land, could allot or sell what was needed to satisfy obligations to Revolutionary War veterans and the government's creditors. Such action, it was hoped, would convince the western settlers that their future lay with the Americans east of the Appalachians.

On April 24, 1784, Congress voted to accept the offer. To exercise control over the area, it had available the US Army, which consisted of three officers and 75 soldiers. Congress authorized a 700-man US Army, and appointed Harmar as its commander. The force would garrison Detroit and other positions the British were to evacuate, prevent unauthorized settlement, and ensure that the Ohio Indians did not disturb authorized settlers.

The Ohio Indians, however, had not been parties to the Treaty of Paris. Congress assigned to Major-General Richard Butler, a prominent Revolutionary War officer, responsibility for negotiating with them treaties that would define acceptable areas of American settlement. In 1784, the Iroquois, who claimed dominion over the Ohio Country, agreed to settlement boundaries in the Treaty of Fort Stanwix, at what is now Rome, New York. In 1785, the Delaware and Wyandot agreed to settlement areas in the Treaty of Fort Mcintosh.

Congress then enacted the Land Ordinance of 1785, which provided that the land available for settlement was to be surveyed, and plots granted or sold. To stop unauthorized settlement, in 1785 the US Army built two outposts: Fort Harmar, at the mouth of the Muskingum River, and Fort Finney, at the mouth of the Miami. The forts' small garrisons, however, soon ceased even trying to stop the flood of settlers occupying empty land.

The ambitious Mohawk leader Joseph Brant (Thayendanegea), who had led pro-British Iroquois in fighting during the Revolutionary War, opposed Butler's efforts. Brant, a well-educated Christian and Freemason, who had friends in the highest ranks of British society, urged the Ohio Indians not to allow individual tribes to negotiate treaties. They should instead act in union to retain control of the area north of the Ohio River, and west of the Muskingum River, either by treaty or by war.

Despite Brant's efforts, Butler persuaded the Shawnee to agree to the Treaty of Fort Finney in 1786. He was unable, however, to persuade other tribes to participate in treaty negotiations. Nor did the treaties terminate raiding by young Indians who wanted scalps, prisoners, horses and plunder.

On September 30, 1785, Richard Butler watched a party of Americans begin to survey the area northwest of the Ohio River. The work, he recorded in his journal, "will eventually, and I think in a short time extinguish the debt of the United States, and fix a permanent prosperity on legal right for millions of people." This monument in East Liverpool, Ohio, marks the location, the "Point of Beginning," from which land boundaries in the United States would be traced as far as the Pacific Ocean. (Author's collection)

An ORDINANCE for the GOVERNMENT of the TERRITORY of the UNITED STATES, North-West of the River Ohio.

This page from the *Journals of the Continental Congress* contains the Northwest Ordinance, with annotations by its drafter, Delegate Nathan Dane of Massachusetts. (Library of Congress, Rare Book and Special Collections Division, Continental Congress & Constitutional Convention Broadsides Collection)

Despite the Indian raiding, the population of Kentucky grew tenfold from 1780 to 1785, to about 40,000. The frontiersmen who had survived the Revolutionary War were soon outnumbered. The new settlers included prominent Virginia Revolutionary War officers. Wealthy land speculators, lawyers, and ambitious politicians soon joined them. The new Kentuckians competed with early leaders such as George Rogers Clark, Daniel Boone, and Simon Kenton for political offices and command of Kentucky militia forces.

In April 1786, Indians killed Colonel William Christian, a prominent Revolutionary War officer who had emigrated to Kentucky in 1785. Governor Patrick Henry of Virginia, whose sister had been left a widow in Louisville, then took action to remedy the problem that Congress had failed to address. He authorized Clark to lead the Kentucky militia on a massive campaign that would destroy the villages from which the Indian raiders came.

Clark assembled 2,000 mounted militiamen to conduct campaigns against Indian villages on the Wabash and Mad rivers. Clark himself led 1,200 mounted men up the Wabash. His campaign soon ended, however, when rival Kentucky officers instigated mutinies. The embittered Clark never again led a Kentucky militia force. Clark's friend Benjamin Logan led the other 800 militiamen against the Mad River villages. His force destroyed Mequachake, near present-day West Liberty, Ohio, and seven other villages. It also killed or discredited several Indian leaders who favored peace.

In 1787, Congress convened in New York under its 12th president, Arthur St Clair, a prominent Revolutionary War leader and large landowner in western Pennsylvania. The future of the United States appeared as bleak as in 1784. The day after Congress convened, Massachusetts militiamen defeated an attack on the state armory by rebels opposed to new taxes. Vermont, to which the defeated rebels fled, was threatening to return to British rule. In Frankland, renamed Franklin, rival governments claimed authority. Soon, fighting broke out between forces loyal to Sevier's independent state, which was considering an alliance with Spain, and those loyal to North Carolina, led by Colonel John Tipton.

On the Ohio River frontier the problem of Indian raiding grew worse. The British, claiming that the Americans had failed to pay debts due under the Treaty of Paris, announced that they would not surrender Detroit. Confident that the United States would soon collapse, they encouraged the emboldened Indians to oppose any American settlement northwest of the Ohio River.

National government under the Articles of Confederation had proven unworkable. Representatives from the 13 states gathered to try to draft a new instrument of national governance. On September 17, 1787, they announced that they had drafted such an instrument, the US Constitution.

The national plan to allot and sell land northwest of the Ohio River had also failed. On July 13, 1787, Congress responded by enacting the Northwest

The prominent Revolutionary War officers who settled at Marietta had commanded most of the Continental Army's New England units. This engraving in Hildreth's *Pioneer History* shows their frontier fortress, Campus Martius. A part of the structure, used as a residence by Brigadier-General Rufus Putnam, survives at the Campus Martius Museum in Marietta, Ohio. (Author's collection)

Ordinance. The legislation, which named the area the Northwest Territory, guaranteed to settlers the same rights that later would be defined in the Bill of Rights of the US Constitution, and established a mechanism by which they could form new states to join the union.

St Clair, appointed by Congress as governor of the territory, acted quickly to commence settlement. A group of prominent Revolutionary War officers, who had organized the Ohio Company, agreed to establish a settlement near Fort Harmar. A second group, the Miami Company, purchased land for settlements near the Miami and Little Miami rivers.

On April 27, 1788, Ohio Company settlers began to build a village at the mouth of the Muskingum River that would be the capital of the Northwest Territory. They named it Marietta, after Queen Marie Antoinette. To protect it, they built the most formidable fortress on the Ohio River frontier, which they named Campus Martius.

To negotiate an end to Indian opposition to American settlement, St Clair proposed a peace council at a neutral site, the falls of the Muskingum River. The proposal received a favorable response from the Ohio Indians. On July 12, 1788, however, Indians attacked soldiers who were building facilities for

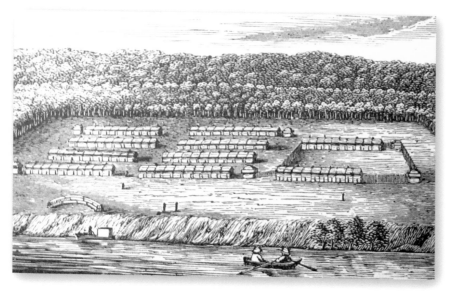

The Gallipolis settlers included the 22-year-old Vicomte de Malartic, who served as an aide-de-camp to St Clair. After receiving two wounds at the battle of the Wabash he returned to France in 1792 to fight for the royalists in the French Revolution. In 1796 he wrote to St Clair of his plans to return to America: "I am very sorry, my dear General, to have left America. I have lost my fortune; the guillotine has deprived me of a great part of my family; the rest are in prison." Malartic later became a prominent general in the French Army. This engraving from Henry Howe's 1847 *Historical Collections of Ohio* shows Gallipolis in 1791. (Author's collection)

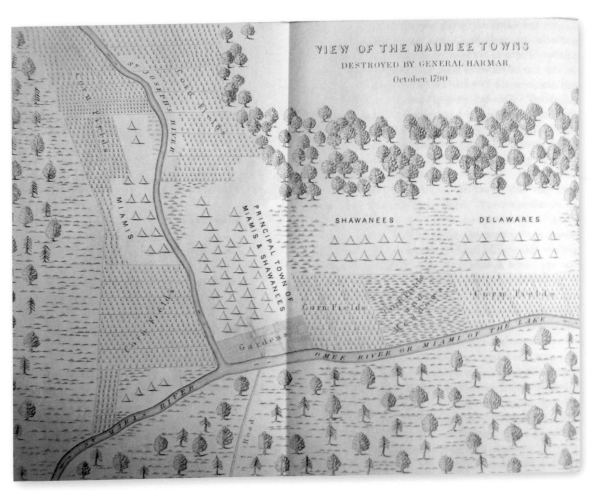

VIEW OF THE MAUMEE TOWNS

DESTROYED BY GENERAL HARMAR,

October, 1790.

This engraving from the *Military Journal of Ebenezer Denny* shows Denny's 1790 map of Kekionga, the largest complex of Ohio Indian villages. Before its destruction in 1790, it contained eight villages with about 250 log or bark-covered structures, surrounded by about 500 acres of cornfields. (Author's collection)

the council, killing two and wounding three at what is now Duncan Falls, Ohio. Outraged, St Clair instead held the council at Fort Harmar. There, in early 1789, some Iroquois, Delaware, and Wyandot chiefs reaffirmed the terms previously agreed to at Fort Stanwix and Fort Mcintosh. Indian raiding, however, continued.

HARMAR'S CAMPAIGN

On April 30, 1789, a new national government assumed power under the US Constitution. Despite Indian attacks, settlement of the Northwest Territory continued. In 1789, Cincinnati and other Miami Company settlements appeared around the new Fort Washington. In 1790, the idealistic Marquis de Lezay-Mamêsia arrived with 450 French nobles and artisans and founded Gallipolis. He hoped that 50,000 more French immigrants would follow, and form an American state.

The new American government, led by President George Washington, was effective in strengthening the United States. Vermont commenced negotiations to join the union as the 14th state. The fighting in Frankland was resolved in a compromise, both sides agreeing that the area should become a federal preserve modeled on the Northwest Territory. It became the Southwest Territory, and in time the state of Tennessee.

In Kentucky, the state militia had continued its war against the Indian raiders. In 1786, Simon Kenton had led a campaign against Chalawgatha, a base for raids near Frankfort, Ohio. In 1787 and 1788, colonels Patrick Brown and John Hardin had led militiamen against villages on the Wabash River. Kentucky leaders told Henry Knox, Washington's Secretary of War, that since 1783 more than 1,500 settlers had been lost in Indian raids. Kentucky constitutional conventions had repeatedly voted against independence. But if the United States wanted Kentucky, it would have to take control of the Northwest Territory.

The new American government authorized Harmar to conduct joint operations with the Kentucky militia against the Indians. It also made it possible for the United States to field a large army on the Ohio River frontier; Congress passed legislation that required the states to provide militia units for US Army campaigns.

On April 20, 1790, the US Army conducted its first offensive operation, a joint action with a force of Kentucky militiamen. Harmar and 120 US Army soldiers joined General Charles Scott and 200 Kentucky militiamen in an attack on Chalawgatha. On May 12, the Indians retaliated, killing five US soldiers and capturing eight at Hartshorne's Defeat, near modern Concord, Kentucky.

Washington then ordered operations on a larger scale. Harmar planned a dual attack against Kekionga, the largest complex of Indian villages in the Ohio Country, at what is now Fort Wayne, Indiana. On September 30 Harmar led 320 US soldiers, three artillery pieces, and 1,133 Pennsylvania and Kentucky militiamen forward from Fort Washington. On the same day, Major John Hamtramck led 50 US soldiers and 280 Kentucky militiamen up the Wabash from Post Vincennes.

Harmar's army burned Kekionga, but suffered heavy losses. On 19 and 23 October the Indians attacked detached units of the American army. At Hardin's Defeat, near Cherubusco, Indiana, and at Kekionga itself, the Indians killed almost 70 American soldiers and more than 100 militiamen. Hamtramck's force, diminished by a militia mutiny, did not reach its destination.

Harmar's campaign was widely considered a failure. In response, moreover, Indian raiders attacked cabins and settlements all across the frontier. On January 2, 1791, they captured the most exposed Ohio Company settlement, killing 12 at the Big Bottom Massacre. On January 8, they besieged the most advanced Miami Company settlement, Dunlap's Station. "Unless government speedily send a body of troops for our protection," the Marietta leader Rufus Putnam wrote to Washington on January 8, "we are a ruined people ... and if we do not fall a prey to the savages, we shall be so reduced and discouraged as to give up the settlement."

The United States, threatened with loss of the Northwest Territory, Kentucky, and perhaps the entire area west of the Appalachians, had no choice but to act. On March 4, 1791, Washington appointed St Clair commander of the US Army. Richard Butler agreed to serve as his second-in-command.

Congress appropriated funds for the army they were to lead, a force of almost 4,000 US soldiers and 1,000–2,000 militiamen. On July 1, that army was to advance from Fort Washington to the site of Kekionga. There, it would build and garrison a fort from which the United States would control the Northwest Territory.

CHRONOLOGY

c.1640–1700   Ohio Country depopulated by Beaver Wars.

1701–55   French and Indian settlement in the Ohio Country.

1755–63   French and Indian War, ending in French surrender to the British of the Ohio Country and the area that will become the Northwest Territory.

1763–64   Pontiac's War.

1764   Beginning of permanent American settlement on the Ohio River frontier.

1774   Lord Dunmore's War.

1775–82   Revolutionary War.

1784

January 14   The United States agrees to the Treaty of Paris; Britain cedes the area that will become the Northwest Territory.

April 24   Congress accepts from Virginia the area that will become the Northwest Territory.

October 22   Iroquois agree to Treaty of Fort Stanwix.

1785

January 1   Delaware and Wyandots agree to Treaty of Fort Mcintosh.

1786

January 31   Delaware, Shawnee and Wyandots agree to Treaty of Fort Finney.

1787

June 21   Congress passes the Northwest Ordinance, which creates the Northwest Territory.

1788

April 27   Marietta, first Ohio Company village, is settled.

June 21   Vote of New Hampshire to ratify US Constitution creates permanent national government for United States.

1789

January 9   Iroquois, Delaware and Wyandots agree to Treaty of Fort Harmar.

April 30   George Washington inaugurated as first US president.

1790

April 20–27   Josiah Harmar leads first US Army campaign, against Chalawgatha on Paint Creek.

September 26 to November 3   Harmar leads second US Army campaign, against Kekionga.

1791

January 2	Indians attack Big Bottom.
January 8	Indians attack Dunlap's Station.
March 4	Arthur St Clair appointed commanding general of the US Army.
March 27	Indians kill 23 US soldiers at Strong's Defeat.
May 2	Indians attack Kirkwood's cabin.
May 15	St Clair arrives at Fort Washington.
May 23 to June 15	Scott expedition against Ouiatenon.
August 1–21	Wilkinson expedition against L'Anguille.
August 14	St Clair orders assembled units to advance to 1st Camp at Ludlow's Station.
September 1	St Clair orders cutting of road to 2nd Camp and construction of Fort Hamilton.
September 11	Last army units arrive at Fort Washington.
October 2	Kentucky militia units, commanded by Oldham, reach Fort Washington.
October 4	The army, commanded by Butler, advances.
October 8	St Clair joins the army at 7th Camp.
October 10	Kentucky militia units join the army at 9th Camp.
October 13	Severe frost kills forage for army and supply horses.
October 14–23	The army constructs Fort Jefferson.
October 17	Failure of flour to reach army requires halving of flour rations.
October 18	First flour convoy arrives.

October 20	First levy units claim that time of service has expired.
October 22	Second flour convoy arrives, allowing further advance.
October 24–29	The army remains at 13th Camp, awaiting flour supplies that will allow further advance.
October 28	Third flour convoy arrives, allowing further advance. Indians leave Kekionga to attack the army.
October 29	More 1st Levy Regiment units leave. Sparks and Piamingo dispatched on scouting expedition.
October 30	The army advances to 14th Camp. Severe storm levels trees.
October 31	60 Kentucky militiamen desert. St Clair dispatches 1st Infantry Regiment to protect advancing flour convoys. Fourth flour convoy arrives, allowing further advance.
November 2	The army advances to 15th Camp.
November 3	Indians and Americans camp on Wabash River.
November 4	Battle of the Wabash. Indians destroy St Clair's army at 16th Camp. Survivors begin retreat.
November 6	American survivors reach Fort Washington.

1794

June 30 to July 1	Battle of Fort Recovery. American defenders repel attack on fort at site of battle of the Wabash.
August 20	Battle of Fallen Timbers. Americans commanded by Anthony Wayne defeat Indian and British militia army.

1795

August 3	Treaty of Greeneville ends Indian war.

OPPOSING COMMANDERS

AMERICAN

Ultimate command of the US Army lay with President George Washington and Secretary of War Henry Knox. **Major-General Arthur St Clair**, the commanding general of the US Army, led the campaign. Born into a rich Scottish family, and trained as a physician at the University of Edinburgh, St Clair had come to America in 1757 as an ensign in the British army. Commended for special bravery at the Plains of Abraham in 1759, he had retired from service as a lieutenant and used his fortune to become a large landowner in western Pennsylvania. At the beginning of the Revolutionary War, St Clair paid from his own funds the cost of recruiting and equipping a

Pennsylvania regiment led by Richard Butler's brother, Colonel William Butler. He then commanded at Fort Ticonderoga, and served as one of Washington's most senior commanders. After a term as President of Congress, he became in 1787 the Governor of the Northwest Territory.

St Clair's staff included his aides-de-camp Lieutenant Ebenezer Denny and Louis de Mauris, Vicomte de Malartic; his adjutant general, Colonel Winthrop Sargent; and his quartermaster general, Samuel Hodgdon. Denny, a 1st Infantry Regiment officer, had served Harmar in the same capacity. Malartic, who had been an officer in King Louis XVI's personal guard, lived in Gallipolis. Sargent, who had served as an artillery officer during the Revolutionary War, was Secretary of the Northwest Territory. Hodgdon had served as Commissary General for the Continental Army.

St Clair's principal subordinate was **Major-General Richard Butler**, the commander of the 1st and 2nd Levy Regiments. Butler, who had been a trader in the Ohio Country before the Revolutionary War, knew personally most of the Shawnee, Delaware, Wyandot, and Mingo commanders. He and the famous Shawnee female chief Nonhelema, also known as the "Grenadier Squaw," had a son, Captain Butler (Tamanatha), who fought at the battle as a Shawnee warrior. After a distinguished career during the war, Butler served as Commissioner for Indian Affairs, and negotiated the treaties of Fort Stanwix in 1784, Fort Mcintosh in 1785, Fort Finney in 1786, and Fort Harmar in 1789.

Major William Ferguson, who commanded the US Artillery Battalion, also served as the army's chief engineer. His principal officers, Captain Mahlon Ford and Captain James Bradford, commanded the battalion's two companies.

St Clair's other senior subordinates led his four infantry regiments. Major John Hamtramck, a Canadian who had fought with the Americans during the Revolutionary War, commanded the 1st Infantry Regiment. His second-in-command, Major David Ziegler, a German immigrant who had fought in the armies of Frederick the Great and Catherine the Great, would later be elected the first mayor of Cincinnati. Only a small unit from the regiment, left to guard baggage, was present at the battle under the command of Captain Thomas Doyle.

Lieutenant-Colonel James Wilkinson was commander of the 2nd US Infantry Regiment. Wilkinson, however, received his appointment too late to join St Clair's army. In his absence, Major Jonathan Heart led the regiment.

This portrait by Frederick Kemmelmayer shows Lieutenant-Colonel William Darke commanding the 1st Levy Regiment at the battle. His wide, cocked hat; single, white belt across his chest; and his sword distinguished him at a distance as an American officer. (Collection of the Museum of Early Southern Decorative Arts, Old Salem Museums and Gardens)

The greatest strength of the American army lay in its extraordinary corps of men like Heart: majors, captains, and lieutenants who had seen years of service in the Continental Army. Thomas Irwin, a wagon driver with the army, wrote of them, "The officers on that campaign was as good as any that ever carried a gun."

The service of Heart's principal subordinate, Captain Robert Kirkwood, had left him a legendary figure. The senior surviving officer of one of the most celebrated units of Washington's army, he led home from the war the remaining men of the Delaware Regiment. They called their commander "the Blue Hen who takes care of his chickens." In his honor, the athletic teams of the University of Delaware would be named the Blue Hens.

Kirkwood led one of the four companies of the regiment present at the battle. Captain Patrick Phelon and Captain Samuel Newman, who had both had distinguished careers during the Revolutionary War, led two other companies. At the time of the battle, Captain Joseph Shaylor, the fourth company commander, had been detached to command Fort Jefferson. In his absence Lieutenant Russell Bissell, Jr, led the unit. Bissell had fought at the battle of Lexington in 1775 as one of the original minutemen.

Lieutenant-Colonel William Darke commanded the 1st Levy Regiment, which by the time of the battle had only two battalions. Major Henry Gaither led the Maryland Battalion. Its four company commanders included Captain Henry Carberry, who had had a distinguished record during the Revolutionary War, and Captain Swearingen. A leading figure on the Ohio frontier, Swearingen was at the time of the battle the Sheriff of Washington County, Pennsylvania.

Darke's other battalion was a consolidation of two that had begun the campaign, the Virginia and Overmountain battalions. By the time of the battle, the Overmountain Battalion, led by Major Matthew Rhea, had been disbanded. Its only remaining unit, a company led by Captain Jacob Tipton, had been consolidated into the Virginia Battalion.

Before the battle, Major George Bedinger, the commander of the Virginia Battalion, had left the army with departing levies from his unit. Captain Nicholas Hannah, whose company was among those that had left, remained and served as temporary battalion commander. His company commanders included Tipton and Captain Joseph Darke, the son of Lieutenant-Colonel William Darke.

Lieutenant-Colonel George Gibson led the 2nd US Levy Regiment. Gibson, a frontiersman like Richard Butler, had three battalion commanders. Major Thomas Butler, a younger brother of Richard Butler, led the Eastern Pennsylvania Battalion. His company commanders included Captain Jacob Slough. A nephew of Gibson, Slough led a scouting expedition the night before the battle.

Major John Clark, another frontiersman, led the Western Pennsylvania Battalion. His company commanders included Captain Edward Butler, a younger brother of Richard and Thomas Butler, and Captain Richard Sparks, who had lived as an adopted Shawnee.

Major Thomas Patterson led the New Jersey Battalion. His company captains included Captain Zebulon Pike, father of the famous explorer. Pike's principal subordinate was Lieutenant Eliakim Littell, who was famous for his exploits as a New Jersey captain during the Revolutionary War.

St Clair's army also had two small mounted units formed by experienced horsemen detached from regular and levy companies. Captain Alexander Truman of the 1st Infantry Regiment led one. Captain Jonathan Snowden of the New Jersey Battalion led the other.

The army also included Pennsylvania and Kentucky militia units. Captain William Faulkner led a company of western Pennsylvania riflemen. Lieutenant-Colonel William Oldham commanded six companies of Kentucky militia. Oldham was at the time the Sheriff of Jefferson County, which included Louisville. His principal subordinate was Major James Brown. His company commanders included Captain Samuel Wells, a famous militia leader, and Captain George Madison, who later would be elected governor of Kentucky.

INDIAN

The Indian army had no formal command structure like that of the Americans. Indian war leaders held their positions solely because others would follow them. None had any power over other commanders or warriors beyond the ability to persuade or embarrass.

A council of such men, which included many of the most famous war leaders in Indian history, agreed on general strategy and tactics. They and

This 19th-century engraving, based on a lost 1797 portrait by Gilbert Stuart, depicts the brilliant Miami commander Little Turtle. After the battle, he opposed further war with the Americans. He died in 1812 at the house of his son-in-law William Wells. Nine years later, his grandson, William Wayne Wells (Wapemongah), would graduate in the first class at the US Military Academy at West Point. (National Anthropological Archives, Smithsonian Institution, BAE GN 00794 06185300)

others then led specific units during the battle. Those units, organized by tribes, commenced the battle in a crescent formation that evolved into a circle surrounding the Americans.

The left horn of the crescent contained the army's Ottawa, Potawatomi, and Ojibwe units. Egushwa, who had succeeded the famous chief Pontiac as Ottawa war leader, led his people. Mad Sturgeon (Nuscotomeg), the best-known Potawatomi war leader of the time, probably led the warriors from that nation. Wapacomegat, who led the Ojibwe, later claimed that he had been the first to reach the Americans at the battle. Younger commanders included the Ottawa Little Otter (Nekeik) and the Potawatomi Main Poc and Blackbird (Nuscotnumeg), who later would become their nations' leading war leaders.

The army's Miami, Shawnee, and Delaware units were in the base of the crescent. **Little Turtle (Mishikinikwa)**, who led the Miami, is sometimes said to have commanded the whole army. He had won fame in 1780 at La Balme's Defeat, near what is now Collins, Indiana. There his Miamis had surrounded and killed 100 French and American militiamen led by French Colonel Augustin La Balme. His fame spread in 1790, when he led Indians who inflicted heavy losses on Harmar's army at Hardin's Defeat and Kekionga. Little Turtle's son-in-law, the younger leader William Wells (Apokonit), commanded at the battle a unit of Miamis. He was the younger brother of Captain Samuel Wells of the Kentucky militia.

Blue Jacket (Waweyapiersenwaw) the leading Shawnee commander, was also sometimes said to have commanded the whole Indian army. He had led the Shawnee who accompanied Bird's Kentucky expedition in 1780. Other important Shawnee leaders at the battle included Black Hoof (Catecahassa), who had commanded the Shawnee at the battle of Peckuwe; Black Fish (Cottawamago); and Captain Johnny (Kekewepelethy).

Buckongahelas was the best-known Delaware commander. Other important Delaware leaders were Captain Pipe (Hopocan), who had commanded the Delaware at Sandusky in 1782, and Big Cat (Whangypushies). During the Revolutionary War, Buckongahelas and Pipe had fought alongside the British, and Big Cat on the American side.

The right horn of the Indian crescent consisted of Wyandot, Mingo and Cherokee units. The best-known Wyandot leader of the time was **Tarhe**, also known as "the Crane." The younger commander Roundhead (Stiahta) would later become the leading Wyandot war leader.

Simon Girty (Katepakomen) led the Mingo. Girty, a Pennsylvania boy captured and raised by the Mingo during the French and Indian War, left a position as an American officer during the Revolutionary War to fight with the British and Indians. Often accused of participating in Indian massacres, Girty was the most hated man on the Ohio River frontier.

John Ward, also known as White Wolf (Wapamowawa), another American who had been captured by the Indians as a boy, probably led the small group of Ohio Cherokee at the battle.

OPPOSING ARMIES

AMERICAN

St Clair's army contained both US Army and militia units. The US Army units were infantry, artillery, and dragoon formations. The infantry units were the 1st and 2nd Infantry regiments, which contained regulars, and the 1st and 2nd Levy regiments, which contained six-month volunteers.

Each regiment, which had an authorized strength of about 950 officers and men, was led by a lieutenant-colonel, and had three battalions. Each battalion, commanded by a major, had four companies. Each company, led by a captain, had an allotted strength of a lieutenant, an ensign, eight noncommissioned officers, a fifer, a drummer, and 66 privates.

St Clair had anticipated having about 3,000 US infantrymen for his campaign. Recruiting failures and the detachment of the 1st Infantry Regiment left him with a smaller number. At the battle he had fewer than 1,300 officers and men in units that contained mere fractions of their authorized complements.

These re-enactors at the reconstructed Fort Steuben in Steubenville, Ohio, give the general appearance of the American regular infantrymen. Because of changes in uniform from 1784–91, and supplies that often did not conform with what had been ordered, the uniforms of St Clair's soldiers often varied in details. The regular infantrymen generally had crossed, white leather belts; blue, knee-length, wool coats with white buttons and linings, and red collars, lapels and cuffs; and white waistcoats and trousers. They had black, wide-brimmed hats, cocked on the left side, with a strip of black bearskin as a crest. The cockades were 4in. circles of black leather, with two parallel, 3in.-long white strips and 6in.-long feathers painted red ornamenting the hats. The artillerymen wore almost identical uniforms, but their coats had yellow buttons and red linings. The levy infantrymen generally had light-brown crossed belts; thigh-length, unlined coats with white buttons, and red collars, lapels and cuffs; white waistcoats; light brown trousers; and plain black, uncocked hats. (Historic Fort Steuben).

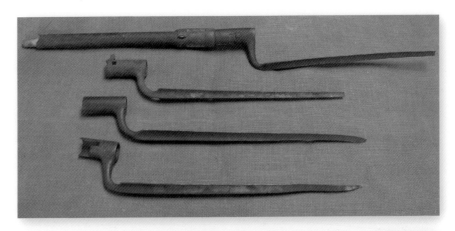

The US infantrymen carried 1766 and 1774 Charleville muskets, provided by France during the Revolutionary War. The .69-cal. weapons, which fired lead balls, could kill men as far away as 1,000yds. Although most men could learn to use their muskets to hit targets the size of a man at about 50yds, the weapons were designed to be fired in mass barrages. Trained men could fire as fast as every 20 seconds. To allow them to load and fire their weapons as fast as possible, the soldiers carried 24 cartridges, which were wrapped paper tubes containing the ball and powder for a single firing. Each musket could be fitted with a bayonet. Those used by St Clair's infantrymen had long metal rings to fit around the musket barrels. When fitted with bayonets, the muskets could be fired, but could not be quickly reloaded.

St Clair's army included two companies of the US Artillery Battalion, and eight field pieces, of which six were used at the battle. Ford's company had 6-pdr guns, 3.66-cal. weapons, usually fired at an elevation of four degrees. Bradford's company had 3-pdr guns of 2.91 caliber. Each gun was operated by a team that consisted of an officer, two gunners, and six soldiers. Each could fire, as often as every 15 seconds, an iron or stone ball, or an exploding shell. Against infantry at close range, 6-pdr guns usually fired tin canisters filled with 56 iron or lead balls, and 3-pdr guns fired canisters with 34 balls.

After a canister dissolved after it was fired, the balls proceeded in an expanding disk. British army tests in 1780 revealed that such a disk from a 6-pdr gun would strike, with about half its balls, a 30yd-wide infantry line 200yds away. The balls had little effect beyond 500yds.

The army also had about 100 men in two mounted units, which were used for reconnaissance, pursuing routed infantry, and guarding the infantry's flanks and the artillery. Men in such dragoon companies usually carried sabers and 1763 Charleville carbines, shorter-barreled muskets that allowed them to function as infantry when dismounted.

St Clair's militia units, which provided additional infantry, were drawn from western Pennsylvania and Kentucky, where adult males constituted both the local electorate and the militia. Led by commanders who recruited volunteers, militia forces were raised for specific defensive or offensive missions, usually for periods not exceeding three months. When insufficient volunteers came forward, men were drafted to fulfill local quotas, and often paid substitutes to fill their places. St Clair's militia infantry was organized into companies, each led by a captain. He had anticipated having a militia force of at least 1,300. At the battle, he had only 320 in one Pennsylvania and six Kentucky militia companies.

The militia units contained men of two types, frontiersmen experienced in fighting Indians and recent immigrants to the West serving as draftees or substitutes. Faulkner's Pennsylvania militia company consisted of experienced frontiersmen. The Kentucky militia companies, however, contained many draftees and substitutes who had only recently arrived in the West.

When Harmar had asked for 1,000 such men for his 1790 campaign, he had assumed that those who would appear would be experienced frontiersmen. On September 18, 1790, however, Ebenezer Denny recorded in his journal, "The Kentucky militia begin to come in; but not such as we had been accustomed to see on the frontier. They appear to be raw and unused to the gun or the woods."

This tomahawk belonged to the frontiersman Joseph Miller, who at the time of the campaign was patrolling the woods near Gallipolis, searching for signs of Indians. (Courtesy of the Portsmouth (Ohio) Public Library)

During the Revolutionary War, Kentucky militiamen, led by commanders such as George Rogers Clark, Benjamin Logan, and Simon Kenton, had learned to conduct successful operations as mounted riflemen. Operating on horseback, these experienced frontiersmen could move without following Indian trails and reach Indian villages without being detected. They could kill or capture Indians while incurring minimal casualties, and retreat quickly to escape peril.

When asked to serve on foot as auxiliary infantrymen in US Army operations, most experienced Kentucky frontiersmen were unwilling to volunteer. The call for volunteers for St Clair's army produced few experienced frontiersmen with rifles. At the battle, more than half of the Kentuckians were recently arrived immigrants, who were given muskets like those of the infantrymen from the army's stores.

The experienced frontiersmen in the militia units carried their own firearms, usually rifles with .40- to .48-cal. barrels, and also tomahawks and knives. Because rifles took twice as long to load, required frequent cleaning, and did not have bayonets, riflemen could not effectively fight massed smoothbore musketry on open battlefields. In experienced hands, however, rifles were deadly weapons. Even minimally competent riflemen could hit targets the size of a man's head at 100yds.

Until a week before the battle, the army included a 42-man rifle company from the Overmountain Battalion of the 1st Levy Regiment. At the battle, the army had 60 riflemen in Faulkner's Pennsylvania militia company, and perhaps another 150 in the Kentucky militia companies and among the civilians. "I … was not disposed," wrote the civilian surveyor Jacob Fowler, "to trust myself among the Indians without my rifle."

The soldiers in St Clair's army varied dramatically in their readiness for combat. The army's highly trained artillerymen were as skilled as any in the world. Some of the infantrymen were veterans of engagements against British units on Revolutionary War battlefields. Others were experienced in fighting Indians on the Ohio frontier. More than half of St Clair's soldiers, however, were strangers in the western wilderness, had never seen battle, and could not use their weapons with even minimal proficiency.

US Army infantrymen were trained in accordance with Major-General Friedrich von Steuben's 1777 *Regulations for the Order and Discipline of the Troops of the United States*. The work, which focused on instruction in how to march and follow orders in battle line, also prescribed training in how to load and fire muskets. It did not, however, require training in marksmanship.

The army's massive logistical failure limited even the instruction that occurred. Because of a shortage of paper to make cartridges, even new recruits for the regular infantry regiments received no practice in actually firing their weapons. "The troops on that campaign," wrote Thomas Irwin, "ought to have been drilled 8 or 10 months and learned them how to handle a gun. I think a number never had handled a gun or shot one."

INDIAN

The Indian army that opposed St Clair, which consisted of volunteers who were free to leave at any time, was likely the largest that had ever been assembled. About 1,400 Indians, generally organized by tribes, commenced the battle in a crescent formation. The tribes were subdivided into smaller units of about 60. Each contained three units of about 20 men.

The tribes spoke languages of two types, Iroquoian and Algonquian. The tribes that spoke Iroquoian languages fought together on the right horn of the crescent. They were Wyandots and Mingo, and a few Ohio Cherokee and Mohawks,

The Wyandots were a product of the Beaver Wars, which destroyed or displaced several groups in southern Ontario that called themselves the Wendat. Those who fled northeast became known as the Huron. Those who fled west, and ultimately settled in Ohio, were called the Wyandot.

The Mingo also were a product of the Beaver Wars. During the seventeenth century, the five tribes of the Iroquois confederacy attempted to incorporate thousands of adopted captives. Many descendants of imperfectly assimilated captives, and of Catholic Mohawks who had separated from their tribe, ultimately moved to Ohio, where they became known as the Mingo.

The Cherokee were a confederacy of groups living in Tennessee and Georgia. They included many groups or subgroups, including the Chickamauga. By 1791, some Chickamauga had migrated north, where they were known as the Ohio Cherokee.

The Algonquian-language speakers included the Anishinabe, a confederacy of the Ojibwe, Ottawa, and Potawatomi, who were usually considered separate tribes. The Ojibwe, often called the Chippewa, had five subgroups. By 1791, the Mississauga, the best known, was widely considered a separate tribe.

The Shawnee, Delaware and Miami, who also spoke Algonquian languages, all had subgroups. Villages named for the Peckuwe, Mequachake, and Chalawgatha subgroups of the Shawnee were the sites of significant battles. By 1791 the Munsee subgroup of the Delaware, and Piankeshaw and Wea subgroups of the Miami, were usually considered separate tribes.

This figure at the Fort Recovery State Museum depicts an Indian warrior dressed in a hunting shirt held in place by a belt. Such men wore loincloths, thigh-high cloth or deerhide leggings attached to their belts by strips of cloth or deerhide, and moccasins. They often had tattoos and nose rings and earrings. For battle, warriors usually removed their shirts and ornaments, covered themselves in bear grease, and used black, red and white paint to decorate their faces and bodies. Indian commanders were indistinguishable from warriors. (Ohio Historical Society, David R. Barker, photographer)

Ohio Indian bows, from 4ft to nearly 6ft long, shot arrows tipped with points made from scrap metal or stone. This bow, displayed at the Clark County Heritage Center in Springfield, Ohio, was used at the battle of Peckuwe in 1780. (Courtesy of Clark County (Ohio) Historical Society)

The Ohio Indians used a variety of smoothbore and rifled firearms of different calibers. Many likely carried the standard weapon used by British infantry, the British Land Pattern Musket. That .75-cal. weapon, often called a "Brown Bess" musket, was generally similar in range, accuracy and reliability to the Charleville muskets of the Americans. The Indians used their muskets to fire multiple projectiles, often rounds of one large ball and three smaller balls of as little as .25 caliber.

By 1791, the Ohio Indians seldom used bows and arrows in war. Such easily portable weapons, however, were useful when supplies of powder or balls were exhausted. Near the end of the battle, some Indians began shooting arrows at the Americans. The weapons, which had a range of about 150yds, could be aimed with slightly better accuracy than smoothbore muskets. For very close combat, most Indians used tomahawks. Some carried wooden clubs, often elaborately carved and decorated, and studded with iron blades. All of them carried knives.

Most of the Indians who fought at the battle were veterans of many engagements. All were well trained in the skills needed for warfare in the Ohio woods. From boyhood they had learned to ignore extremes of temperature, to endure hunger and thirst, and to survive alone for indefinite periods. At age 12 they began training in combat skills and small-unit maneuvers. At age 14 they began participating in raids.

The Indians were usually merciless enemies, who fought the Americans just as they fought one another. Their experience of war had been in conflicts that often ended in groups' extermination. In battle, they tried to kill or capture as many members of an enemy group as possible, regardless of age or sex. They also sought to intimidate potential enemies by demonstrating the spectacular savagery that any foes could expect at their hands.

The Indians preserved in varying degrees ancient customs regarding the treatment of captives, who became the property of the warriors who took them. Prisoners were usually adopted or enslaved. Adult males, however, and also females, were often tortured to death, and sometimes ritually eaten. By 1791 many Ohio Indians had abandoned such practices. The Wyandot, Mingo, Delaware and Shawnee usually sold captives who were not adopted to traders or British officers. The prisoners then, by periods of labor, repaid their purchase price, and obtained funds for travel home.

Other Indians, however, had not reformed. In 1790 the Wyandot chief Tarhe stopped some visiting Ohio Cherokee from burning a captured American woman at a Wyandot village. In 1791, Indians tortured to death a man captured near Dunlap's Station. After the battle of the Wabash, John Brickell, the adopted son of the Delaware chief Big Cat, saw the remains of a dead American far from the field. A Delaware warrior told him that Ojibwe, whom the Delaware considered "brutes," had eaten the man.

When seen for the first time by Americans in peaceful settings, the Indians did not appear formidable. Lieutenant Ebenezer Denny changed his mind after fighting them. They were, he wrote, "an enemy brought up from infancy to war, and perhaps superior to an equal number of the best men that could be taken against them."

ORDERS OF BATTLE
NOVEMBER 4, 1791

(00) Estimated number in unit
(K) Killed or fatally wounded
(W) Wounded
(NP) Not present

AMERICAN (1,700)[1]

Major-General Arthur St Clair, Commander
    Major-General Richard Butler, Second-in-Command (K)

Lieutenant Ebenezer Denny, 1st Infantry Regiment, Aide-de-camp
Louis de Mauris, Vicomte de Malartic, Aide-de-camp (W)
Colonel Winthrop Sargent, Adjutant General (W)
Samuel Hodgdon, Quartermaster General (NP)

1ST US INFANTRY REGIMENT (5) [2]
Major John Hamtramck, Commander (NP)
Major David Ziegler, Second-in-Command (NP)
Captain Thomas Doyle, Acting Commander (W)

2ND US INFANTRY REGIMENT (235)
Lieutenant-Colonel James Wilkinson, Commander (NP)
Major Jonathan Heart, Acting Commander (K)
    Company of Captain Robert Kirkwood (K)
    Company of Captain Samuel Newman (K)
    Company of Captain Patrick Phelon (K)
    Company of Captain Joseph Shaylor (NP), Lieutenant Russell Bissell, Jr, Acting Commander

US ARTILLERY BATTALION (60)
Major William Ferguson, Commander (K)
    Company of Captain Mahlon Ford (W)
    3 x 6-pdr guns
    Company of Captain James Bradford (K)
    3 x 3-pdr guns

1ST US LEVY REGIMENT (350)
Lieutenant-Colonel William Darke, Commander (W)

MARYLAND BATTALION (200)
Major Henry Gaither, Commander (W)
    Company of Captain William Buchanan (W)
    Company of Captain Henry Carberry
    Company of Captain Benjamin Price (K)
    Company of Captain Van Swearingen (K)

COMBINED VIRGINIA AND OVERMOUNTAIN BATTALION (150)
Major George Bedinger, Commander (NP)
    Captain Nicholas Hannah, Acting Commander
    Company of Captain Joseph Brock
    Company of Captain Joseph Darke (K)
    Company of Captain Jacob Tipton (K)

2ND US LEVY REGIMENT (630)
Lieutenant-Colonel George Gibson, Commander (K)

EASTERN PENNSYLVANIA BATTALION (210)
Major Thomas Butler, Commander (W)
    Company of Captain William Power
    Company of Captain William Purdy (K)
    Company of Captain Jacob Slough (W)
    Company of Captain John Smith (K)

WESTERN PENNSYLVANIA BATTALION (240)
Major John Clark, Commander (W)
    Company of Captain Edward Butler
    Company of Captain Johann Cribbs (K)
    Company of Captain John Guthrie (K)
    Company of Captain Richard Sparks (NP), Lieutenant George Lukens, Acting Commander (K)

NEW JERSEY BATTALION (180)
Major Thomas Patterson, Commander
    Company of Captain Zebulon Pike
    Company of Captain William Piatt (K)
    Company of Captain Jonathan Rucastle

COMPANIES OF DRAGOONS (100)
Captain Alexander Truman, Commander (W)
    Company of Captain Alexander Truman (W)
    Company of Captain Jonathan Snowden (W)

RIFLE COMPANY OF PENNSYLVANIA MILITIA (60)
Captain William Faulkner, Commander

COMPANIES OF KENTUCKY MILITIA (260)[3]
Lieutenant-Colonel William Oldham, Commander (K)
Major James Brown, Second-in-Command
    Company of Captain James Ellis
    Company of Captain Presley Gray (K)
    Company of Captain James Lemon (K)
    Company of Captain George Madison (W)
    Company of Captain John Thomas (W)
    Company of Captain Samuel Wells

INDIAN (1,400)[4]

LEFT HORN OF CRESCENT (400)

OTTAWA (150)
Egushwa, Commander

OJIBWE (150)
Wapacomegat, Commander

POTAWATOMI (100)
Mad Sturgeon, Commander

BASE OF CRESCENT (700)

MIAMI (100)
Little Turtle, Commander

SHAWNEE (300)
Blue Jacket, Black Hoof, Black Fish, and Captain Johnny, Commanders

DELAWARE (300)
Buckongahelas, Captain Pipe, and Big Cat, Commanders

RIGHT HORN OF CRESCENT (300)

WYANDOT (200)
Tarhe and Roundhead, Commanders

MINGO (75)
Simon Girty, Commander

CHEROKEE (25)
John Ward, Commander

NOTES

1 On November 3, Colonel Winthrop Sargent recorded the army's numbers as 1,380 US Army officers and men, and 319 militia officers and men. On November 17, he calculated the total number of officers and men present on November 4 as 1,669. Except for the 2nd Infantry Regiment, the numbers in individual units are estimates.

2 Only a 1st Infantry Regiment baggage guard was with the army at the time of the battle.

3 There may have been five Kentucky militia companies; some sources suggest that George Madison may have been a lieutenant in another commander's company.

4 Estimates of the numbers of Indians have ranged from 500 to 2,000. William Wells said in 1804 that there had been about 1,400. The numbers for tribes are based on his 1793 estimates of the warriors tribes could provide to oppose Wayne's army.

OPPOSING PLANS

AMERICAN

St Clair's orders were to build a fort at Kekionga, and to maintain there a permanent garrison of at least 1,200 men. To reach his objective from Fort Washington with artillery, he had to advance on a road. Construction of such roads in the wilderness required felling trees to foot-high stumps, and building log bridges across ravines and unfordable streams.

St Clair had available the road that Harmar had used for his 1790 campaign. By using parts of two roads built during the Revolutionary War, Clark's Trace and Bird's War Road, Harmar had created a circuitous, 170-mile-long route. By using it his army had reached Kekionga in 18 days and returned to Fort Washington in 13.

From the best available information, St Clair estimated that Kekionga was about 115 miles from Fort Washington. A large, permanent garrison at Kekionga would require massive supplies. A road 55 miles shorter than Harmar's would allow supplies to reach the fort in 2–3 days' less time, and significantly reduce the danger that an American garrison might starve. Although construction of a shorter route would significantly delay his advance, St Clair decided to build a direct road to Kekionga, with forts at intermediate points along it.

Exhaustion of food supplies, St Clair believed, would be the greatest danger the advancing American army would encounter. The army's contractors were to deliver to Fort Washington the supplies for 365,000 daily rations of a half-pound of beef and a half-pound of bread. As the army advanced, his officers and men would consume about 4,000 rations a day. The army would take with it a herd of about 300 oxen to provide the beef, and also the flour for 90,000 rations of bread.

The remaining flour would be transported forward during the campaign. Wagons could carry large loads of flour, but could not easily be used on rough, ungraded roads in the wilderness. Wagons, and artillery carriages and caissons, might need eight horses or oxen to pull uphill, and dozens of men with ropes to allow safe descent. Even when the vehicles moved slowly, their fragile axles and wheels often collapsed. They were used only when necessary.

Packhorses, which could carry 200lb loads about 25 miles a day, would transport most of the army's supplies and its continuing resupplies of flour. About 800 horses provided by contractors would carry the flour. Convoys of packhorses, each carrying the flour for 45,000 rations, would advance every five days from fort to fort, and ultimately from the farthest fort to the army.

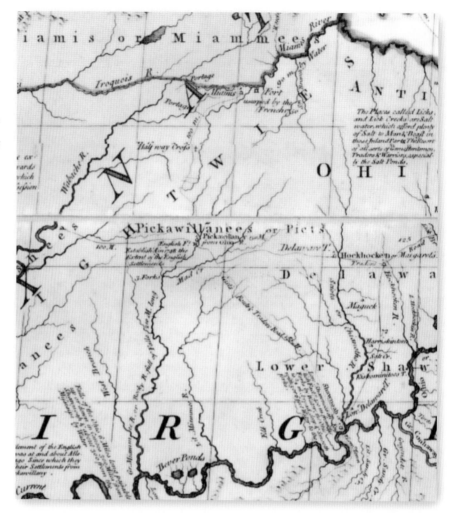

During border negotiations for the Treaty of Paris, the British and Americans used a 1774 map by the cartographer John Mitchell. This detail shows the locations of Fort Washington, below "Bever Ponds" at the bottom center, and Kekionga, just above "Fort usurped by the French" at the top center. St Clair, who had no better map of the area, estimated that Kekionga was 17 degrees west of north, and 115 miles from Fort Washington. It was actually 14 degrees west of north, and 141 miles from Fort Washington. (Library of Congress, Geography and Map Division)

The horses, however, like the oxen, required their own food. That could not be supplied by packhorses, which could carry only about a six-day supply of food for themselves. St Clair's army, as dependent upon forage as a modern army on fuel, would starve if its animals could not find food by grazing.

The Indians, St Clair believed, were a much less significant threat. They were not likely to attack a large army, especially one protected by artillery. They had not attacked Harmar's army, only two detached forces. Any Indian attack, moreover, would be against the army while it marched or was encamped. The US Army's operational handbook, Steuben's *Regulations*, specified how commanders were to reshape such an attack into a conflict between opposing battle lines. In such lines, American soldiers would fight in battalions, with each company occupying about 30yds, and the men deployed in two ranks. American soldiers were to march in at least two columns, more than 100yds apart. The men in each column were to proceed in two files. If attacked, a two-file column was to become a two-rank battle line, or would retire to the parallel column, where a stronger battle line could be formed.

American camps were to be rectangles. The battalions that would form the army's front and second lines in battle were to occupy a camp's two long sides. St Clair formed his camps by shifting 90 degrees the army's columns of march, with one column forming his camps' front sides, and the other their rear.

American lines of communication and supply

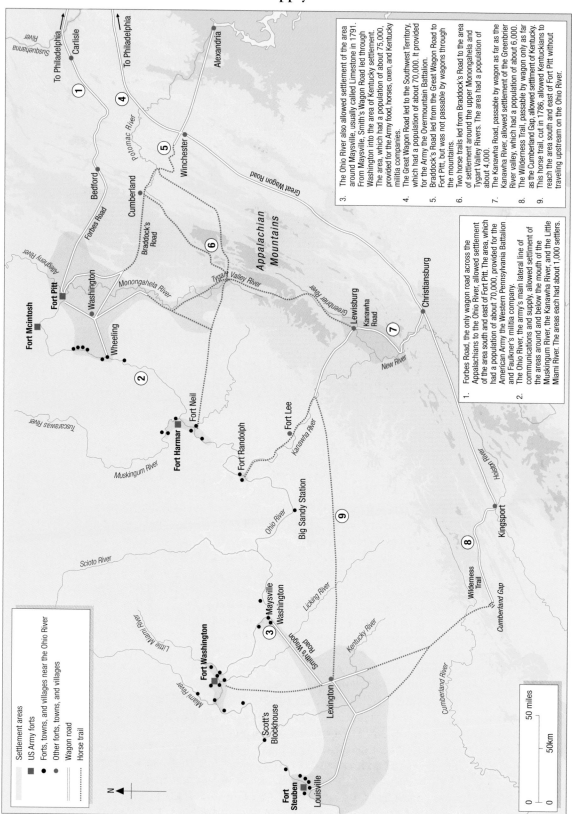

3. The Ohio River also allowed settlement of the area around Maysville, usually called Limestone in 1791. From Maysville, Smith's Wagon Road led through Washington into the area of Kentucky settlement. The area, which had a population of about 75,000, provided for the Army food, horses, oxen, and Kentucky militia companies.

4. The Great Wagon Road led to the Southwest Territory, which had a population of about 70,000. It provided for the Army the Overmountain Battalion.

5. Braddock's Road led from the Great Wagon Road to Fort Pitt, but was not passable by wagons through the mountains.

6. Two horse trails led from Braddock's Road to the area of settlement around the upper Monongahela and Tygart Valley Rivers. The area had a population of about 4,000.

7. The Kanawha Road, passable by wagon as far as the Kanawha River, allowed settlement of the Greenbrier River valley, which had a population of about 6,000.

8. The Wilderness Trail, passable by wagon only as far as the Cumberland Gap, allowed settlement of Kentucky.

9. This horse trail, cut in 1786, allowed Kentuckians to reach the area south and east of Fort Pitt without traveling upstream on the Ohio River.

1. Forbes Road, the only wagon road across the Appalachians to the Ohio River, allowed settlement of the area south and east of Fort Pitt. The area, which had a population of about 70,000, provided for the American Army the Western Pennsylvania Battalion and Faulkner's militia company.

2. The Ohio River, the army's main lateral line of communications and supply, allowed settlement of the areas around and below the mouth of the Muskingum River, the Kanawha River, and the Little Miami River. The areas each had had about 1,000 settlers.

33

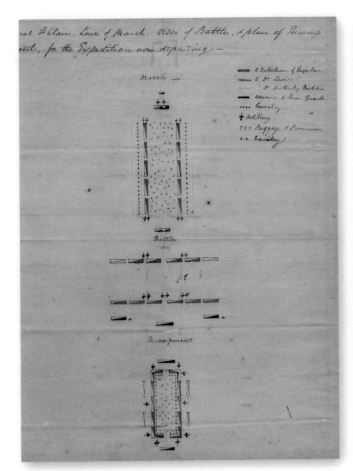

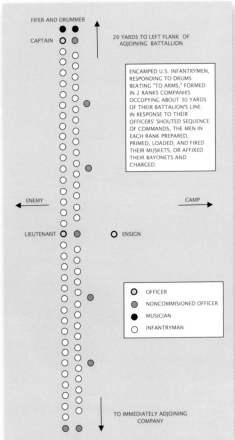

FIFER AND DRUMMER
CAPTAIN

20 YARDS TO LEFT FLANK OF ADJOINING BATTALION

ENCAMPED U.S. INFANTRYMEN, RESPONDING TO DRUMS BEATING "TO ARMS," FORMED IN 2 RANKS COMPANIES OCCUPYING ABOUT 30 YARDS OF THEIR BATTALION'S LINE. IN RESPONSE TO THEIR OFFICERS' SHOUTED SEQUENCE OF COMMANDS, THE MEN IN EACH RANK PREPARED, PRIMED, LOADED, AND FIRED THEIR MUSKETS, OR AFFIXED THEIR BAYONETS AND CHARGED.

ENEMY

CAMP

LIEUTENANT

ENSIGN

○ OFFICER
◑ NONCOMMISIONED OFFICER
● MUSICIAN
○ INFANTRYMAN

TO IMMEDIATELY ADJOINING COMPANY

LEFT

On September 27, 1791, Richard Butler received St Clair's orders on how the army was to march, encamp and form lines of battle, which were graphically explained by this sketch drawn by St Clair's aide-de-camp, Lieutenant Ebenezer Denny. (Courtesy of the Ohio Historical Society)

RIGHT

From 1777 to 1812, Steuben's *Regulations* prescribed how US Army infantrymen conducted operations. The *Regulations* specified in exact detail where the officers and men in each company were to camp and where they were to stand in the battle line. This drawing shows the proper location in a battle line for the officers and men of a company on a battalion's far right. (Author's collection)

March and encampment doctrines incorporated a basic assumption of 18th-century European military thought: that armies were machines that generated firepower. The amount depended upon the discipline of its soldiers. If American soldiers immediately obeyed the sequences of commands prescribed in Steuben's *Regulations*, they would generate the greatest firepower their weapons could produce.

Experienced militia commanders conducted operations against the Indians with different assumptions. Their orders of march and encampment were designed to minimize initial casualties, avoid encirclement, and reshape an attack into a battle of attrition between dispersed forces protected by the thick western woods. Militiamen usually advanced in a long column in single file. Militia camps were squares, which occupied as much ground as possible.

In 1778, General Lachlan Mcintosh, leading an army to build Fort Laurens, encamped 1,300 men in squares containing nearly 40 acres. If Indians attacked one of Mcintosh's camps, Colonel James Smith recalled, "each officer was immediately to order the men to face out and take trees… and in this form they could not take the advantage of surrounding us, as they commonly had done when they fought the whites."

At the battlefield, the Americans would encamp as Steuben's *Regulations*, not militia doctrines, prescribed. A US Army force larger than Mcintosh's would form a rectangle on 7 acres of high ground. They would be ready to form two battle lines as quickly as possible. The three battalions in each line would oppose any attack with a storm of lead and iron. St Clair's lines had only a fraction of the strength that he had anticipated. They nonetheless could produce devastating firepower. Operating at maximum efficiency, and using canister shot, the three guns in his front line could fire canisters containing 170 balls every 15 seconds, and the three in the second line could fire canisters with about 100. The 600 infantrymen in each line, with each rank firing three times a minute, could fire about 300 balls every ten seconds, or charge with almost 600 bayonets.

In actual battle conditions, the lines would not operate with such efficiency. Nor could the muskets long maintain such a rate of fire without overheating. St Clair nonetheless was confident that his army's firepower could overcome any force the Indians could field.

INDIAN

Communication and logistical restraints limited the ability of the Indians to oppose St Clair's army. They could not quickly assemble a large force, nor maintain it for more than a few days far from sources of food supply. They also could not fight long with firearms unless the British provided supplies of powder. St Clair's campaign offered an opportunity to inflict on the Americans a demoralizing defeat. If the Americans advanced slowly, the Indians could assemble an army large enough to offer battle. If they advanced far enough, the Indians could use that army on a field close to their bases of supply. If the British provided sufficient food and powder, the Indian army would be able to fight effectively.

To casual observers, an Indian army appeared to fight as a disorganized horde of undisciplined, cowardly combatants. That appearance, however, was deceptive. "As they are a sharp, active kind of people," wrote Colonel James Smith, who had lived for four years as a Mingo, "and war is their principal study, in this they have arrived at considerable perfection."

Indian assumptions about the nature of war and the effectiveness of operations were very different from those of the Americans. In war, the Indians' goal was to avoid losses while killing or capturing as many enemies as possible. They measured success in operations by two criteria, the number of casualties incurred and the number inflicted. The Indian experience of war was of conflict between small groups. Indian operational doctrines therefore emphasized above all minimizing casualties. Warriors, who fought dispersed, always retreated when an enemy advance was likely to cause significant loss. Even successful engagements were terminated whenever casualties reached an unacceptably high level. Indian commanders, Smith wrote, never attacked without "the sure prospect of victory, and that with the loss of a few men: and if at any time they should be mistaken in this, and are likely to lose many men by gaining the victory, it is their duty to retreat, and wait for a better opportunity of defeating their enemy."

Enemies were to be attacked only when they could not fight on even terms. Any tactic that would reduce enemy combat power was employed. Enemy commanders were always targeted. Deceit was used whenever possible. When Indians applied their doctrines in battle, they appeared to their enemies to be almost invisible. They remained unseen, concluded Colonel Bouquet, the only British commander to defeat them in a large engagement, because they always followed three tactical rules. "The first," he observed, "that their general maxim is to surround the enemy. The second, that they fight scattered, and never in a compact body. The third, that they never stand their ground when

The area of operations

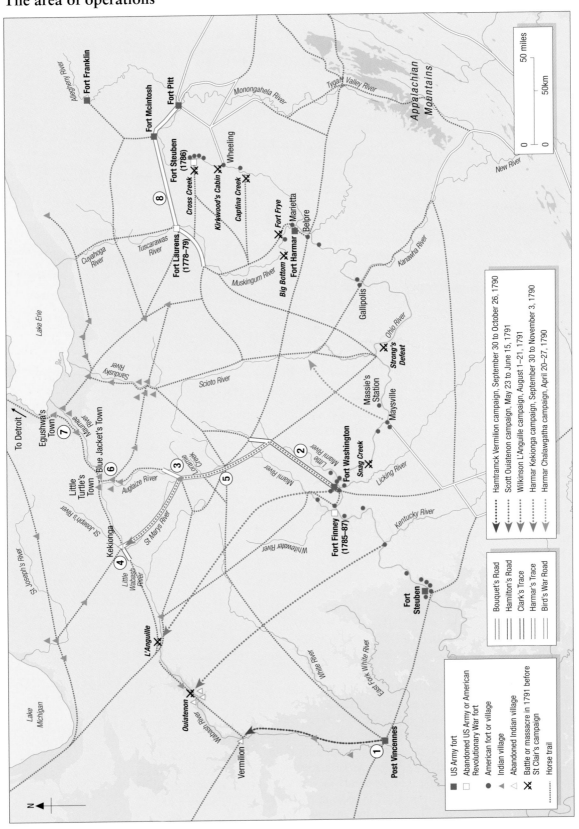

Legend

US Army fort ■

Abandoned US Army or American Revolutionary War fort □

American fort or village ●

Indian village ▲

Abandoned Indian village △

Battle or massacre in 1791 before St Clair's campaign ✕

Horse trail ⋯

Bouquet's Road

Hamilton's Road

Clark's Trace

Harmar's Trace

Bird's War Road

Hamtramck Vermilion campaign, September 30 to October 26, 1790

Scott Ouiatenon campaign, May 23 to June 15, 1791

Wilkinson L'Anguille campaign, August 1–21, 1791

Harmar Kekionga campaign, September 30 to November 3, 1790

Harmar Chalawgatha campaign, April 20–27, 1790

50 miles
50km

Map labels

Fort Franklin

Allegheny River

Fort Mcintosh

Fort Pitt

Monongahela River

Tygart Valley River

Appalachian Mountains

Fort Steuben (1786)

Cross Creek

Kirkwood's Cabin

Captina Creek

Wheeling

New River

Cuyahoga River

Tuscarawas River

Fort Laurens (1778–79)

Fort Frye

Marietta

Belpre

Fort Harmar

Big Bottom

Muskingum River

Kanawha River

Lake Erie

Sandusky River

Scioto River

Gallipolis

Ohio River

Strong's Defeat

Egushwa's Town

To Detroit

Maumee River

Blue Jacket's Town

Massie's Station

Maysville

Little Turtle's Town

Auglaize River

Loramie Creek

Miami River

Little Miami River

Fort Washington

Snag Creek

Licking River

St Joseph's River

Kekionga

St Marys River

Whitewater River

Fort Finney (1785–87)

Kentucky River

Little Wabash River

L'Anguille

Lake Michigan

Ouiatenon

Wabash River

Vermilion

White River

East Fork White River

Fort Steuben

Post Vincennes

N

attacked, but immediately give way, to return to the charge." The result, he wrote, was that a commander attacked by Indians would "find himself surrounded by a circle of fire, which, like an artificial horizon, follows him everywhere."

The Indians had tested their tactics in centuries of war with one another, and almost 40 years of war against British and American regulars as well as French, Spanish, and American militia forces. In planning their attack on St Clair's army, the Indians could draw upon their experience in six prior engagements with large British or American forces on the Ohio River frontier. At Monongahela in 1755 they had destroyed a 1,300-man British army led by General Edward Braddock, in what is now Braddock, Pennsylvania. At Grant's Defeat in 1758, a British army of 800 led by Major James Grant had met a similar end in what is now Pittsburgh. Those battles had revealed the vulnerability in the western woods of forces that generated musket firepower in battalion formations.

At Bushy Run in 1764, however, the Indians had learned the power of bayonet charges. After surrounding a British army of 500 led by Bouquet, they had pursued men apparently fleeing a collapsing part of the British perimeter. A force concealed by Bouquet had then ambushed the pursuing Indians in a devastating bayonet charge.

In three more-recent battles, the Indians had faced militia forces, which used tactics similar to their own. At Point Pleasant in 1774 the Indians had trapped a force of 1,100 militiamen against the Ohio and Kanawha rivers, but had been forced to withdraw because of high casualties. At Peckuwe in 1780, a smaller Indian force, attacked by a 1,000-man army with artillery, had fled before being encircled. At Sandusky in 1782 the Indians had surrounded a force of 500 American militiamen, which had broken through the encirclement and fled.

The defeat of St Clair's army presented a formidable tactical challenge. No Indian commander had ever tried to encircle with so many warriors such a large enemy force. Nor had any ever attacked a camp defended by artillery. The Indians, however, guided by British advice on how to silence the American guns, were confident that the tactics that had prevailed against Braddock's and Grant's superior firepower would overcome St Clair's as well.

This statue in Barberton, Ohio, depicts the Delaware Captain Pipe, one of the leading Indian commanders. Almost 60 in 1791, Pipe had fought at Monongahela. He later said that he had personally taken several American scalps at the battle of the Wabash. (Jonathan Reed Winkler)

MAP NOTES

1   Americans settled at Post Vincennes among earlier French settlers.
2   Clark's Trace, built to transport artillery for George Rogers Clark's 1780 Peckuwe campaign, led from the site of Fort Washington to the site of the Indian village.
3   Bird's War Road, built to transport artillery for British Captain Henry Bird's 1780 Kentucky campaign, crossed the portage between Loramie Creek and the Auglaize River. A second Bird's War Road, in Kentucky, led south from the Licking River.
4   Hamilton's Road, built to transport artillery for British Lieutenant-Colonel Henry Hamilton's 1779 campaign against Post Vincennes, crossed the portage from Kekionga to the Little Wabash River.

5   Harmar's Trace, built for Harmar's 1790 campaign against Kekionga, followed Clark's Trace, cut a new road to Bird's War Road, and cut another new road to Kekionga.
6   After the destruction of Kekionga in 1790, most of the inhabitants relocated to this area at the mouth of the Auglaize River, known as The Glaize.
7   Here, at the Foot of the Maumee Rapids, the British delivered supplies to the Indians by ship.
8   Bouquet's Road, built for British Colonel Henry Bouquet's 1764 campaign against the Ohio Indians, led from Fort Pitt to the mouth of the Tuscarawas River, and was last used in 1779 as far as Fort Laurens.

THE CAMPAIGN AND BATTLE

THE AMERICAN ADVANCE

From March 4–27, 1791, Secretary of War Henry Knox and St Clair planned the campaign, as Secretary of the Treasury Alexander Hamilton made arrangements for the United States to finance its cost. The supplies needed for the campaign were determined and ordered. Letters were dispatched to Revolutionary War veterans offering them commissions as officers. Plans for recruiting the army's soldiers were designed.

St Clair was to await the army at Fort Washington. Butler was to go to Fort Pitt, organize the arriving men and supplies, and forward them down the Ohio River. The other officers who accepted appointments were to disperse across the United States to recruit soldiers. The army was to consist of the existing 1st Infantry Regiment and the US Artillery Battalion, a new 2nd Infantry Regiment, two regiments of levies, militia units, and allied Indians. Soldiers for the 1st and 2nd Infantry Regiments would enlist for two years and be recruited in the New England states, New York, Delaware, North Carolina, and South Carolina. Soldiers for the two levy regiments would enlist for only six months, the anticipated time needed for the campaign.

This 1868 Benson Lossing engraving is based on Major Jonathan Heart's 1791 sketch of Fort Washington, the head-quarters of the US Army from 1790 until 1793. (Author's collection)

LEFT
This surviving portion of Forbes Road passes through woods near Murrysville, Pennsylvania. (Courtesy of the Murrysville Historical Preservation Society, photograph by Joan Kearns)

RIGHT
This modern replica of a flatboat is at the Ohio River Museum in Marietta, Ohio. (Author's collection)

Those for the 1st Levy Regiment were to come from Maryland, Virginia, and the Southwest Territory, and those for the 2nd Levy Regiment from New Jersey and Pennsylvania. Kentucky would provide about 1,500 militiamen, and western Pennsylvania a smaller number. The Americans also hoped that friendly Senecas in New York, or Chickasaws in Mississippi, might provide small auxiliary forces or scouts.

On March 28 St Clair left Philadelphia for Fort Washington. Two days later, the previously healthy commander was stricken with gout. The condition left even the slightest pressure on his toes, ankles, wrists or shoulders unbearably painful.

As he painfully traveled the 850 miles to his destination, the officers he would lead accepted their commissions. Most had been celebrated commanders during the Revolutionary War. They agreed to serve as captains and lieutenants, hoping that service would lead to rapid promotion, or offer an opportunity to see the western country where many planned to settle. A few obtained commissions by political influence. Lieutenant Winslow Warren, the son of Mercy Warren, and Ensign David Cobb, Jr, the son of the Speaker of the Massachusetts House of Representatives, became officers in Phelon's company of the 2nd Infantry Regiment. Both would fall at the battle. Ensign William Henry Harrison, whose father had signed the Declaration of Independence, received an appointment in the 1st Infantry Regiment, and served in the garrison at Fort Washington.

The assembly of the army, the first American national effort, created an atmosphere of patriotism in which old offenses and rivalries were forgotten. In Maryland, Henry Carberry, one of the leaders of the Pennsylvania soldiers who had threatened Congress in 1783, was offered a captain's commission in the Maryland Battalion. In the Southwest Territory, John Sevier, now general of the territorial militia, was active in recruiting an "Overmountain Battalion" for the 1st Levy Regiment. John Tipton's son Jacob, who had led men against Sevier three years before, recruited a company for the unit.

St Clair's journey led to Carlisle, the boyhood home of Richard Butler. From there the 268-mile-long Forbes Road went west through the mountains. On that narrow road, most of his soldiers would march to war. On its rough path, often moving at only 1–2 miles an hour, wagons would carry the supplies they would use in 3–4-ton loads.

In mountain valleys, he rode through Bedford, the last American town with the amenities of what St Clair called "the Atlantic world," and then past the abandoned British Fort Ligonier and his nearby home. Beyond the

The beginning of the campaign, January 8 to October 4, 1791

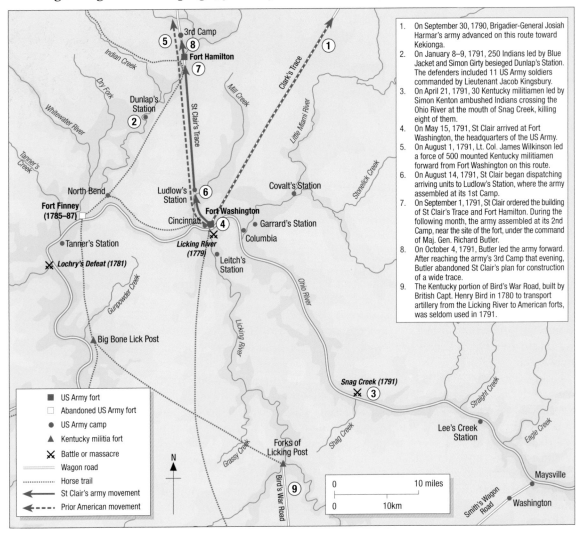

1. On September 30, 1790, Brigadier-General Josiah Harmar's army advanced on this route toward Kekionga.
2. On January 8–9, 1791, 250 Indians led by Blue Jacket and Simon Girty besieged Dunlap's Station. The defenders included 11 US Army soldiers commanded by Lieutenant Jacob Kingsbury.
3. On April 21, 1791, 30 Kentucky militiamen led by Simon Kenton ambushed Indians crossing the Ohio River at the mouth of Snag Creek, killing eight of them.
4. On May 15, 1791, St Clair arrived at Fort Washington, the headquarters of the US Army.
5. On August 1, 1791, Lt. Col. James Wilkinson led a force of 500 mounted Kentucky militiamen forward from Fort Washington on this route.
6. On August 14, 1791, St Clair began dispatching arriving units to Ludlow's Station, where the army assembled at its 1st Camp.
7. On September 1, 1791, St Clair ordered the building of St Clair's Trace and Fort Hamilton. During the following month, the army assembled at its 2nd Camp, near the site of the fort, under the command of Maj. Gen. Richard Butler.
8. On October 4, 1791, Butler led the army forward. After reaching the army's 3rd Camp that evening, Butler abandoned St Clair's plan for construction of a wide trace.
9. The Kentucky portion of Bird's War Road, built by British Capt. Henry Bird in 1780 to transport artillery from the Licking River to American forts, was seldom used in 1791.

mountains, the road led past abandoned Hannastown, burned by the Indians nine years before, and Bushy Run, where Bouquet had defeated the Indians in 1764. At the end of Forbes Road he reached Fort Pitt on the Ohio River.

St Clair then traveled more comfortably, moving down the Ohio from settlement to settlement. By the river, his soldiers and supplies would reach Fort Washington on flatboats. Floating wooden boxes, from 40–60ft long and 10–20ft wide, they moved down the river at the rate of the current, about 2–3 miles per hour.

St Clair's river journey led past isolated cabins and many scenes of Indian warfare. From Fort Pitt, attacked in 1763, he went 96 miles downstream to Wheeling, attacked in 1777 and 1782, and Mcmechen's Narrows, where Indians had slaughtered militiamen in 1777. About 85 miles on lay Marietta and Fort Harmar, and, 15 miles beyond, Belpre and Fort Neil. After another 85 miles he reached Gallipolis; nearby Fort Randolph, a Virginia militia fort attacked in 1778; and the field of the 1774 battle of Point Pleasant.

Another 150 miles brought St Clair to Massie's Station, and the site of Hartshorne's Defeat the year before. Some 12 miles ahead lay Maysville.

In 1789 Captain Robert Kirkwood settled on land in what is now Bridgeport, Ohio. On May 2, 1791, 40 Indians attacked his cabin, and suffered heavy casualties. Kirkwood's son later built this house on the site of the cabin in which he and his father had lived. (Brianna Parrish)

After another 58 miles, he reached Columbia, the first of the Miami Company settlements, 8 miles upstream from Fort Washington.

On the banks of the river, St Clair had seen the remains of burned cabins. And at the forts and settlements he learned of the fighting that had recently occurred. On March 11 the Indians had attacked Fort Frye on the Muskingum. On March 27 they had killed 25 US soldiers at Strong's Defeat. On April 21, 30 Kentuckians led by Simon Kenton had killed eight Indian raiders at the mouth of Snag Creek. On May 2, 15 men led by the famous Revolutionary War veteran Robert Kirkwood had killed more at Kirkwood's Cabin.

On May 15, St Clair at last reached Fort Washington and its 100-man garrison. Built from planks from disassembled flatboats, it was shaped as a rough square with 180ft-long sides and corner blockhouses. Cincinnati, just southwest of the fort, had grown in two years into a village of 40 log cabins, four taverns, and about 250 inhabitants. There, a settler recalled, "the Indians had now become so daring as to skulk through the streets at night and through the gardens around Fort Washington."

From Fort Washington to Fort Hamilton

Losses on Harmar's campaign, at Strong's Defeat, and by expiration of enlistment terms, had reduced the 1st Infantry Regiment to only 299 noncommissioned officers and men. Around that core, St Clair would build his army. He ordered the commanders at the army's forts to assemble their men at Fort Washington.

The Kentuckians were unwilling to wait until July to commence operations. On May 23, after promising that he would provide another force for St Clair's campaign, Major-General Charles Scott, the commander of the Kentucky militia, led 750 mounted militiamen forward from Scott's Blockhouse at the mouth of the Kentucky River. The Indians, who assumed that the Kentuckians would attack Kekionga, assembled a force of 1,000 warriors there.

Scott, however, deceived the Indians. Avoiding horse trails to escape detection, the Kentuckians instead attacked another complex of villages,

Ouiatenon. There the Kentuckians killed 30 Indians, captured 42, burned several villages and destroyed hundreds of acres of growing corn. On June 15, without suffering any casualties, Scott's force reached Fort Steuben. The Indians, outraged at their losses, demanded that the British provide munitions and food for the fighting to come. The British agreed. Supplies would arrive at the foot of the Maumee Rapids, where the Maumee River ceased to be navigable by ships.

At Fort Pitt, Butler received reports of Indian attacks almost daily. Cabins were burned within 2 miles of the fort. Fort Lee on the Kanawha River was besieged. In May, Indians killed five militiamen and wounded two at Captina Creek. In June, the famous militia captain Larson Van Buskirk fell at Cross Creek. As settlers demanded that detachments of soldiers be sent to protect them, officers arrived with understrength units, or sent word of delays as they tried to persuade men to enlist for the low pay offered. Supplies appeared in mislabeled containers, or in an unusable condition. Butler was deluged by complaints that the gunpowder was defective, the uniforms and shoes unwearable, and the packhorse saddles and tents useless.

At Fort Washington, similar problems overwhelmed St Clair. As settlers demanded soldiers to guard their forts and stations, flatboats arrived from Fort Pitt with supplies, and ferryboats brought horses, oxen and men from Kentucky. In workshops around Fort Washington, men labored to repair broken muskets, build wagons, and manufacture leather harnesses, as others awaited paper to make cartridges and brass for horse bells.

Samuel Hodgdon, the army's Quartermaster General, was responsible for such matters. Hodgdon, however, was still in Philadelphia. Colonel Winthrop Sargent, the secretary of the Northwest Territory, volunteered to help by serving as the army's adjutant general. St Clair and Sargent then tried to bring order to a chaos of arriving contractors and artisans, officers and recruits, horses and oxen, boxes, bags, and barrels.

By June 27, when companies of the Maryland Battalion of the 1st Levy Regiment and New Jersey Battalion of the 2nd Infantry Regiment arrived at Fort Washington, the July 1 date for commencing the campaign had been

abandoned. More units continued to arrive until July 15, when boats with 1st Infantry Regiment companies appeared. Weeks then passed with no further arrivals; a drought had left the Ohio River too low for safe navigation above Wheeling.

Some 500 Kentucky mounted militiamen, led by Lieutenant-Colonel James Wilkinson, had arrived at Fort Washington for the campaign. Unwilling to wait, they insisted on commencing a second operation. On August 1, Wilkinson led them northwest to the Miami River, and up Sevenmile Creek toward Kekionga. Like Scott, he deceived the Indians by avoiding horse trails, and attacked another complex of villages, L'Anguille. There, the Kentuckians killed six and captured 34 while losing two killed and one wounded. They then went down the Wabash to Ouiatenon, burned the crops that had survived Scott's fires, and returned to Kentucky on August 21.

Wilkinson had found few Indians at L'Anguille. Most had gone to the foot of the Maumee Rapids where, as British ships delivered the promised munitions and food supplies, the Indians held a council to plan their response to St Clair's invasion. Joseph Brant and a delegation of Indian leaders left with the ships to seek additional military aid and diplomatic support. They were to return by September 1 with whatever additional help the British would provide.

On August 14, St Clair ordered the fragment of his army that had arrived to advance 5 miles to Ludlow's Station, where there was sufficient forage for the army's horses. From Ludlow's Station, the site of the army's 1st Camp, surveyors were to lay out the course of his trace for 18 miles to the Miami River. There he would construct a fort that could be supplied by boat up the Miami, which he would name Fort Hamilton.

On August 29, flatboats began to arrive at Fort Washington again. St Clair sent the arriving units forward to the 1st Camp. He ordered the men already there to build the trace to the Miami River, prepare the army's 2nd Camp there, and begin construction of Fort Hamilton.

As more units arrived, St Clair rode to Lexington to arrange for the militia units that would advance with his army. He wanted at least 1,000 men who would serve on foot. There he heard more bad news. Scott, despite promises that his and Wilkinson's campaigns would not diminish the force available to St Clair, was having trouble finding commanders and men willing to serve unmounted. St Clair returned to Fort Washington to find that Butler, Hodgdon, and a large convoy of flatboats had finally arrived. On September 11, the last officers and men from Fort Pitt appeared. St Clair sent the new arrivals on to the 2nd Camp, where construction of Fort Hamilton had begun.

The luckless American general then encountered new obstacles. The skies, so long cloudless, began to deliver torrential downpours of rain. What St Clair described as "the heaviest rains that were ever known to fall with such continuance," made work on the fort impossible. The army's tents offered no refuge. "Poured in sheets and torrents all night!" Captain Samuel Newman wrote in his journal on September 24. "Damned the economy of the contractor for the thinness of our tents … through which the rains beat, as if through a sieve." The new arrivals, moreover, had brought with them an epidemic of flu. Sickness spread through the army. "At present," Newman wrote on October 3, "I am the only captain in our regiment who is well enough to do duty."

This portrait by Charles Willson Peale depicts Lieutenant-Colonel James Wilkinson. After emigrating to Kentucky in 1784, he won popularity by traveling to New Orleans and securing from the Spanish an agreement that allowed Kentuckians to use the Mississippi River. He failed, however, to disclose another agreement, by which he had become a Spanish spy. Appointed commander of the 2nd Infantry Regiment, he received his commission too late to join St Clair's army. He would later become commanding general of the US Army. (Independence National Historical Park)

This portrait by an unknown artist depicts Major James Brown. In 1782, he and his brother, John Brown, emigrated to Kentucky. As St Clair traveled to Fort Washington, John Brown, a Virginia Congressman. carried $10,000 to Lexington to pay the expenses for the Kentucky militiamen who were to participate in the campaign. Both brothers then served in Scott's and Wilkinson's campaigns. James Brown would later be a US senator for Louisiana, and US ambassador to France. John Brown would be a US senator for Kentucky. (US Senate Historical Office)

As soon as Fort Hamilton was built, Butler was to lead the army north. On September 27, St Clair gave him orders on how the army was to proceed. It was to march in two columns, on two parallel, 40ft-wide roads, 250yds apart. It was to encamp in rectangles, with the army's columns forming the camps' long sides.

St Clair himself returned to Lexington to arrange for Kentucky militia units to join the army. There, before returning to Fort Washington, he learned that the Kentuckians would number only a few hundred. On October 2, about 350, led by Lieutenant-Colonel William Oldham and Major James Brown, arrived at Fort Washington. The army St Clair would have, less than half the size he was promised, was at last ready to advance.

The army's readiness for the campaign did not impress those who had reached Kekionga the year before. Lieutenant Ebenezer Denny, who had served as Harmar's aide-de-camp, wrote in his journal on September 26 that Harmar "predicted a defeat. He suspected in me a disposition to resign; discouraged the idea. 'You must,' said he, 'go on the campaign; some will escape, and you may be among the number.'"

From Fort Hamilton to Fort Jefferson

On October 4, 23-year-old Tecumseh and six other Shawnee warriors concluded their last raiding expedition of the season by ambushing a party of Americans herding cattle from Clarksburg to Marietta. After killing four men and a ten-year-old boy, they moved north to join the army that would oppose the American advance.

That same day, the Americans on the Miami River went forward. At daylight, as Steuben's *Regulations* prescribed, the drums beat "the General," the order to strike tents and prepare to march. Across the Miami, which was almost too high to ford, two openings in the woods marked the points from which the dual paths of St Clair's Trace would proceed. Their straight course led directly toward a 300ft-high hill 2 miles away.

The soldiers, shivering in their light uniforms, soon discovered that the army's 1,000 horses had been left free to wander in the woods. By noon, the horses had been retrieved. The drums beat "Assembly," and then "March."

This detail from an 1891 print by Lucien C. Overpeck depicts Fort Hamilton. Shaped as an irregular rectangle about 1,000ft in circumference, it had four blockhouses. (Author's collection)

The American advance, October 5 to November 3, 1791

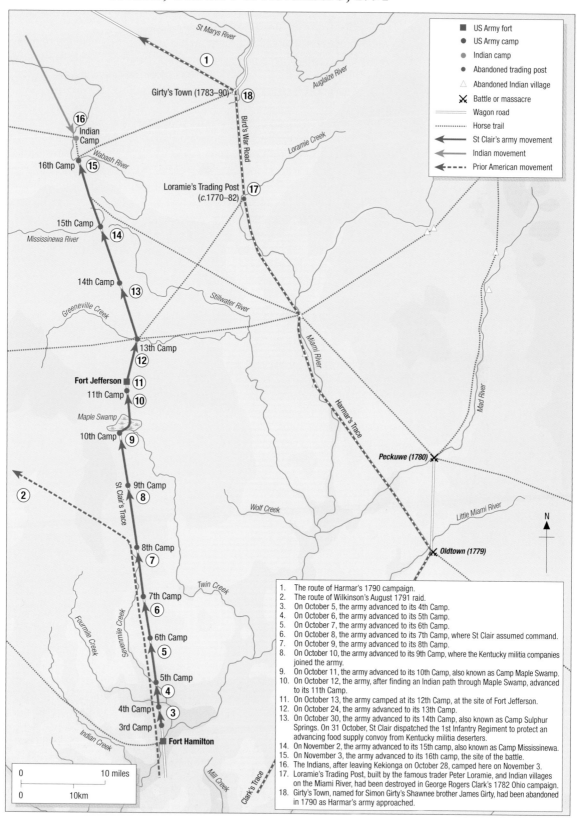

Legend:
- ■ US Army fort
- ● US Army camp
- ● Indian camp
- ● Abandoned trading post
- △ Abandoned Indian village
- ✗ Battle or massacre
- ═══ Wagon road
- ⋯⋯ Horse trail
- ⬅━ St Clair's army movement
- ⬅━ Indian movement
- ⬅┅ Prior American movement

St Marys River

Auglaize River

Girty's Town (1783–90) ①⑱

Bird's War Road

⑯ Indian Camp

16th Camp ⑮

Wabash River

Loramie Creek

Loramie's Trading Post (c.1770–82) ⑰

15th Camp ⑭

Mississinewa River

Stillwater River

14th Camp ⑬

Greeneville Creek

Miami River

Mad River

13th Camp ⑫

Fort Jefferson ⑪

11th Camp ⑩

Maple Swamp

10th Camp ⑨

Peckuwe (1780) ✗

9th Camp ⑧

St Clair's Trace

②

Wolf Creek

Little Miami River

N

8th Camp ⑦

Twin Creek

Oldtown (1779) ✗

7th Camp ⑥

Swanmile Creek

6th Camp ⑤

5th Camp ④

Fourmile Creek

4th Camp ③

3rd Camp

Indian Creek

Fort Hamilton

Mill Creek

Clark's Trace

Scale:
0 ――――― 10 miles
0 ――――― 10km

1. The route of Harmar's 1790 campaign.
2. The route of Wilkinson's August 1791 raid.
3. On October 5, the army advanced to its 4th Camp.
4. On October 6, the army advanced to its 5th Camp.
5. On October 7, the army advanced to its 6th Camp.
6. On October 8, the army advanced to its 7th Camp, where St Clair assumed command.
7. On October 9, the army advanced to its 8th Camp.
8. On October 10, the army advanced to its 9th Camp, where the Kentucky militia companies joined the army.
9. On October 11, the army advanced to its 10th Camp, also known as Camp Maple Swamp.
10. On October 12, the army, after finding an Indian path through Maple Swamp, advanced to its 11th Camp.
11. On October 13, the army camped at its 12th Camp, at the site of Fort Jefferson.
12. On October 24, the army advanced to its 13th Camp.
13. On October 30, the army advanced to its 14th Camp, also known as Camp Sulphur Springs. On 31 October, St Clair dispatched the 1st Infantry Regiment to protect an advancing food supply convoy from Kentucky militia deserters.
14. On November 2, the army advanced to its 15th camp, also known as Camp Mississinewa.
15. On November 3, the army advanced to its 16th camp, the site of the battle.
16. The Indians, after leaving Kekionga on October 28, camped here on November 3.
17. Loramie's Trading Post, built by the famous trader Peter Loramie, and Indian villages on the Miami River, had been destroyed in George Rogers Clark's 1782 Ohio campaign.
18. Girty's Town, named for Simon Girty's Shawnee brother James Girty, had been abandoned in 1790 as Harmar's army approached.

This engraving from the *Military Journal of Ebenezer Denny* shows Lieutenant Ebenezer Denny, who served both Harmar and St Clair as aide-de-camp, and would later be elected the first mayor of Pittsburgh. Denny, who admired both his commanders, named his two sons Harmar and St Clair. (Author's collection)

This portrait by Luella Walter Eisenlohr, based on a portrait by Gilbert Stuart, depicts Colonel Winthrop Sargent. Sargent, known during the Revolutionary War as the "best-dressed man in the Continental Army," would later be the first Governor of the Mississippi Territory. (Collection of the Museum of Mississippi History, Mississippi Department of Archives and History)

Butler then led the army forward. After 20 paces, he shouted "Support arms," the order allowing men to advance in less precise order. The Americans then waded through three feet of water into the woods.

George Adams, the army's chief scout, and other frontiersmen led the way. As surveyors determined the course to Kekionga, hundreds of men took two-hour turns felling trees with the army's 80 axes and one crosscut saw. As they cleared the paths, others marked the miles from Fort Washington with wooden stakes.

The Americans marched forward to the sound of fifes and drums. Far to the left and right of the paths, dragoons and riflemen guarded the army's flanks. On each path, about 1,000 soldiers marched, teams of horses pulled the army's artillery carriages and caissons, along with supply and baggage wagons. Between the paths, hundreds of oxen and horses were herded forward. With them went hundreds of civilians, the men employed as scouts, surveyors, horsemasters, and herdsmen, and the women employed as cooks, seamstresses, and washerwomen. There were also many children.

The mile-long procession stopped every few hundred yards. "The woods, Sargent wrote in his journal, "were everywhere so compact as made the opening of a road extremely tedious. Bridges were frequently to be thrown over streams and ravines, and the infantry, though marching by single files, were necessitated to cut their way at every step." That evening the Americans formed their 3rd Camp, a large square within which the horses and oxen were confined to graze. The army had advanced 2 miles.

On October 5, St Clair sent Oldham's militiamen forward from Fort Washington. On October 7 he rode north to take command. Harmar, who watched St Clair leave to join the untrained army, did not envy his successor. "It was a matter of astonishment to him," wrote Denny, "that the commanding general, who was acknowledged to be perfectly competent, should think of hazarding, with such people, and under such circumstances, his reputation and life, and the lives of so many others."

St Clair reached Fort Hamilton that evening. There he learned that no flour convoy was preparing to advance to the army. His frustration grew as he rode farther the next day. At the army's 3rd Camp, his 40ft-wide paths ended. A single, 12ft-wide road led on. Before reaching the army's 7th Camp that evening he rode past Oldham's advancing Kentuckians and three more square camps. In five days, the army had advanced less than 20 miles.

St Clair was furious at the slow progress. And on a single road and in square camps, he told Butler, the army could not form battle lines quickly if attacked. Butler explained that, if he had followed St Clair's orders, the army could not have advanced as fast as it had. The men had too few axes to cut a path wider than the minimum needed for horses to pull the carriages, caissons, and supply wagons. If allowed to wander, the oxen and horses took hours to collect before the day's march could begin. He had therefore used square camps, which provided enough internal pasture for a night's grazing.

St Clair's fury grew into alarm when he talked with Hodgdon. The absence of flour convoys, the Quartermaster General told him, would soon be a serious problem. The army, Hodgdon admitted, had only a small fraction of the 90,000 flour rations it was to carry as it advanced. The army's flour supply, St Clair calculated, would be exhausted by October 18, and the beef from the oxen by November 5. He sent orders to Fort Washington to advance flour for the army immediately. He sent with the orders 290 of the army's supply horses for use by the contractors in transporting the flour.

After a prayer service on Sunday, October 9, St Clair led the army forward on the single path the axmen could cut. Moving through flatter and lower country, the army was able to advance 12 miles in two days. After it reached its 9th Camp on October 10, Oldham's Kentuckians arrived. St Clair, who considered the militiamen an auxiliary force, ordered them to camp separately, behind the army toward Fort Washington.

On Tuesday, October 11, after advancing 6 miles, the army reached an area where further progress on the surveyor's line to Kekionga became impossible. A scout's horse sank 3ft into flooded ground before being rescued. As men searched for routes around Maple Swamp, the army halted at its 10th Camp.

On October 12, Butler found an Indian trail on elevated ground to the east. The army followed it 6 miles to its 11th Camp. That night, the weather turned bad. Since leaving Fort Hamilton, the Americans had marched in dry, cold weather, a relief after the torrential rains. On October 13, however, they awoke to find a layer of ice atop the water in their containers. A day of cold rain followed the first hard frost.

At a spring a mile ahead, St Clair decided to built a second fort, which would be named Fort Jefferson. There, at its 12th Camp, the army stopped on October 13. When Butler gave the usual order to form a square camp, St Clair countermanded the order. Because of the frost, there would no longer be enough food within a camp for the horses and oxen to eat. The army would now camp as St Clair had originally ordered.

On Friday, October 14, the men assembled as usual, a half-hour before daylight, for review in their battalion ranks. Wet after a night sleeping on mud in their porous tents, and cold in their light clothing, they stood in a hard rain in disintegrating shoes as they were told about the work to come. A total of 200 men were to cut trees and build the fort; 700 more were detailed to find food for the horses and oxen. Some searched the woods for places where forage was still available, and led the animals there. Others gathered weeds and carried them back to the camp.

Four days and nights of cold rain followed, as the wet soldiers labored and shivered in their tents. No convoy arrived. On October 17, St Clair announced that there would be only half-rations of flour. The deficit would be offset by more of the almost inedible beef available from the army's starving oxen. The army's standard rations provided barely enough nourishment for soldiers serving in fort garrisons. For freezing men laboring in the woods, half-rations were grossly inadequate. Three regular US Army infantrymen were caught trying to desert. Levies and militiamen began disappearing into the woods.

On October 17, six weeks after they had promised, Brant and the Indians who had left the foot of the Maumee Rapids returned. The site was deserted. After receiving the munitions and supplies the British had delivered, the Indians had moved to Kekionga to await St Clair's arrival. Brant, instead of joining them, returned to Ontario.

On October 18, when the rain turned to hail, a packhorse convoy finally arrived at the 12th Camp. It carried enough flour to feed the army for two days. Half-rations of flour would continue. The levies in Captain Nicholas Hannah's Company of the Virginia Battalion announced that, by their calculations, their time of service would expire in another two days. Other levies said that their terms would also end soon.

Wednesday, October 19, was the tenth anniversary of Cornwallis's surrender at Yorktown. There was, however, no celebration at the 12th Camp. St Clair's gout was worse than ever. Butler was also ill. Many of the officers were barely on speaking terms. The regulars had offended the levy officers by trying to persuade them to enlist in regular units. Both had offended the militia officers by refusing to recognize their ranks. Most of the officers disliked Sargent. Lieutenant-Colonels William Darke and George Gibson both claimed to be the ranking levy officer. Darke detested Major John Hamtramck. The lack of supplies had left Hodgdon a pariah.

Desperate to get the flour needed for a further advance, St Clair ordered Oldham to lead his militia force back down the trace to escort advancing convoys. If sent back toward Kentucky, Oldham told St Clair, his freezing, starving men would not return. St Clair instead sent Captain William Faulkner's Pennsylvania militiamen.

On Thursday, the hail continued. The men of Hannah's Company announced that it was time for them to leave. The Virginians then went down the trace with Faulkner's militiamen, leaving Hannah, who chose to remain. On Friday, October 21, the miserable men building Fort Jefferson and collecting weeds awoke to find atop the water in containers a layer of ice a half-inch thick. No Indians had been seen. "It seems," the puzzled general wrote in a report to Knox, "somewhat extraordinary that they should have allowed us to be here so long in the interior of their country and never looked at us."

On Saturday, 20 Kentucky militiamen deserted. A new company of 60 Kentuckians, however, led by Captain James Ellis, arrived with a second packhorse convoy. Like the militiamen who had deserted, most of the men in Ellis's company were draftees. Garret Burns, a 21-year-old Irish immigrant who worked as a hatter, was among them. As a paid substitute for a draftee, he had fought in a militia company at Kekionga in 1790. In Ellis's company, Burns remembered, "I was directed to act as sergeant, having had some experience, compared with the rest, in Indian warfare."

The convoy was small, St Clair was told, because there weren't enough packhorses. Unable to find forage, many of the horses at Fort Washington, Ludlow's Station, and Fort Hamilton had died. Most of the others were too weak to carry loads. St Clair sent Hodgdon back to Fort Washington to address the problem, and with his Quartermaster General most of the army's remaining supply and baggage horses.

On Sunday, Fort Jefferson was finally completed. St Clair reluctantly assembled the army to watch as two of the US soldiers who had tried to desert the prior Monday were hanged. Butler asked the American commander to let him advance quickly to Kekionga with 1,000 men while it was still possible. St Clair refused. The army, however, could not remain at its 12th Camp. No more food for the horses and oxen could be found in the area. The army must either retreat, or advance in the hope that flour supplies would soon arrive. St Clair ordered that it would advance.

From Fort Jefferson to the battlefield

Monday, October 24, was the first dry and relatively warm day the army had experienced since arriving at its 12th Camp 11 days before. St Clair left Captain Joseph Shaylor at Fort Jefferson with two artillery pieces and 120 men, most of whom were too ill to march. The rest of the army, about 2,050 officers and men, and perhaps 200 civilians, advanced almost 6 miles to Greenville Creek. St Clair, who could neither ride nor walk, was carried forward in a sling strung between two horses.

When the army arrived at its 13th Camp, St Clair ordered a halt until further food supplies arrived. The following day he assembled his officers. Although no Indians had been sighted, the American commander reviewed his plans in the event of a battle. "The savages," he told his officers, "if violently attacked will always break and give way and when once broke, for the want of discipline, will never rally." The officers, he said, must convince their men "that if they stand and fight like soldiers, certain victory will be their reward."

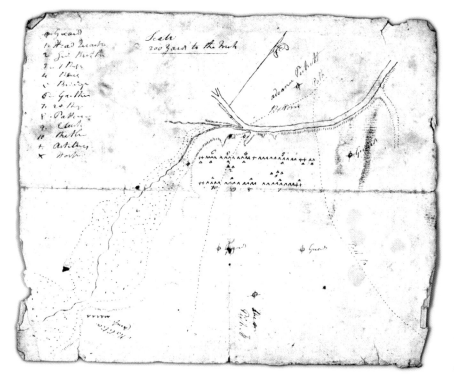

This drawing by an American officer shows the army's 13th Camp, where about 2,000 men camped in a rectangle with a front side more than 1,000yds long. The drawing shows the army's eight battalions arrayed on the camp's front and rear sides, with the Maryland Battalion, Virginia Battalion, Overmountain Battalion, and 1st Infantry Regiment in the front line; the Eastern Pennsylvania Battalion, Western Pennsylvania Battalion, New Jersey Battalion, and 2nd Infantry Regiment in the rear line; and the artillery at the camp's corners and at the center of the front line. (Clements Library, University of Michigan)

While touring Independence Hall in 1796, Piamingo met the Shawnee chief Blue Jacket, who was also visiting Philadelphia. They asked the Americans to mediate an end to the long war between their peoples. This statue of Piamingo by William Beckwith is in Tupelo, Mississippi. (Courtesy of William Beckwith)

On October 26, as the hungry Americans continued to await the arrival of a convoy, the weather worsened. Rain resumed, and then turned to snow. Fearful that the Kentucky militiamen might desert, he ordered them to move their camp ahead of the army, across the creek.

On Thursday, October 27, as the army consumed the last of its flour, more levies announced that their terms of service were about to expire. On the same day, many of the Americans saw Indians for the first time. Led by the famous chief Piamingo, 20 Chickasaws arrived from their villages in Mississippi. They had come at the request of Sevier to provide scouts for the army. The Chickasaws, Sargent recorded in his journal, "have the most inveterate animosity to all the Indian tribes northwest of the Ohio … and have been at war with the whole of them from time immemorial."

There was also an encouraging report. A third flour convoy was a day's distance from the army. It would, Sargent recorded in his journal, "enable us to move forward for a few more marches. Beyond that our prospects are gloomy; no magazines established, and even an uncertainty of supply at Fort Washington, with the difficulties of transportation every day increasing by the season and to become still greater, as we add to our distance… But the general is compelled to move on, as the only chance of continuing our little army."

On Friday, as hail and snow fell, the third packhorse convoy arrived. Its 74 horses carried enough flour to feed the army for four more days. They also brought a supply of coats for the 1st Infantry Regiment. Told that any who enlisted in the regiment for two years could have a coat, 39 freezing levies accepted the offer.

On Saturday, October 29, Majors George Bedinger and Matthew Rhea led most of the remaining levies from the Virginia and Overmountain Battalions back to Fort Washington, where the two battalion commanders were to arrange for their men's pay and transportation home. The departing units included a 42-man Overmountain Battalion company of riflemen, which had protected one side of the army's camp. The departure left Darke, the commander of the 1st Levy Regiment, with a three-battalion unit in which the Virginia Battalion had only two companies, and the Overmountain Battalion only one. The Overmountain battalion company, Captain Jacob Tipton's, was incorporated into the Virginia Battalion, which Hannah would command until Bedinger returned.

Many of St Clair's officers, fearing the approach of worse weather, urged him to end the campaign. He should, they said, retreat, build an intermediate fort between Fort Hamilton and Fort Jefferson, and resume the campaign in the spring. St Clair, however, was determined to accomplish his mission. Kekionga, he believed, was only about 40 miles ahead. Because there had been no hint of Indian opposition, he thought that only an advance to Kekionga would be needed. To confirm that there was no Indian army assembled to oppose him, he sent Captain Richard Sparks, who had lived in Ohio as a Shawnee, forward with Piamingo and the Chickasaws on a long-range scouting mission.

There were, messengers reported, two advancing flour convoys. To hasten the arrival of the flour, he sent back with the departing levies every horse that

LEFT
This monument now marks the site of the army's 14th Camp, also known as Camp Sulphur Springs. (Robert Hart)

RIGHT
This monument now marks the site of the army's 15th Camp, also known as Camp Mississinewa. (Robert Hart)

the army could spare. To ensure that, once it arrived, the army could advance rapidly, he sent all equipment and baggage that was not indispensable back to Fort Jefferson, and 300 men forward to cut the trace as far ahead as possible.

On October 30, the army marched forward again, with St Clair still in his sling. Because the horses were too weak to carry their usual loads, the army's tents and much of its baggage had to be abandoned beside the trace. Each man had to carry his own share of the remaining flour, enough for three days. After 7 miles, the army reached its 14th Camp.

On Monday, October 31, the Americans arose after a sleepless night. A terrifying storm had swept through, uprooting large trees and felling huge branches. As the army was sending horses back to retrieve its abandoned tents and baggage, Oldham reported that 60 hungry Kentuckians had deserted and were moving back down the trace. The deserters, St Clair feared, might take the flour carried by the advancing convoys. He sent to save his food supply the army's strongest and most reliable unit. Hamtramck and Major David Ziegler led the 300 men of the 1st Infantry Regiment back down the trace.

That evening, St Clair received the best news since leaving Fort Washington. Protected by Faulkner's riflemen, a fourth supply convoy arrived at the 14th Camp. Its 212 horses brought a 12-day supply of flour and a herd of 100 cattle, enough for the army's final advance. The axmen had cut the trace for miles ahead. The army would be able to move quickly.

St Clair's gout, however, had become intolerable. Hoping that it might improve with rest, he waited another day to march. That night Darke wrote a letter to his wife, which he dispatched with soldiers returning to Fort Washington. "We have been crawling through Indian country," he wrote, "I expect we shall march early on towards the Indian towns, where we, I believe, shall not find an Indian"

On Wednesday, November 2, as it snowed again, the army marched on. Scouts reported that they had found a small stream that flowed west 7 miles ahead. At last, St Clair and his officers concluded, the army had reached a waterway that led to Lake Erie rather than the Ohio River. The army advanced to the stream, the Mississinewa River, the site of its 15th Camp.

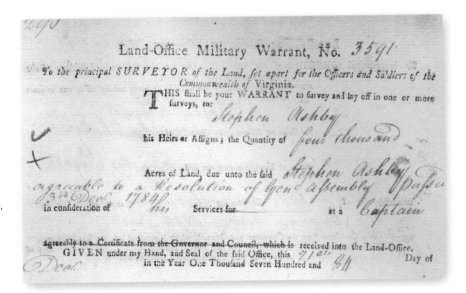

On November 3, as the army marched forward again, there was more good news, which seemed to vindicate St Clair's decision to continue the campaign. About 3 miles beyond the Mississinewa the army reached an Indian trail, which led in the direction of Kekionga. About 4 miles farther, scouts reported, the trail crossed a large stream flowing west. That, the American officers concluded, was the St Marys River, and Kekionga was about 15 miles downstream.

The army halted as St Clair met with his senior officers to consider the significance of the trail and stream. Around a fire that had been lit by Thomas Irwin, a civilian wagon driver, they also discussed other news. The scouts who had found the stream had seen a party of 15 Indians just beyond it. The report disturbed Oldham, who thought that they might be scouts for an Indian army. The officers also received other reports of Indians sighted beyond the army's flanks, and of evidence that Indians had passed in large numbers. "The general," Irwin recalled, "observed that he did not think that the Indians were watching the movements of the army with a view to attack them. The officers present concurred with him in that opinion."

St Clair ordered the army to advance to the stream. There the army would spend the night at its 16th Camp, and the following day move swiftly without further pause to Kekionga, The site for encampment was a 400yd-wide area of high ground overlooking the stream. It was, Sargent would write three months later, "certainly so defensible against regular troops that I believe any military man who has not had the fatal experience of the late misfortune would unhesitatingly have pitched upon it. It is, however, (I must confess) surrounded by close woods, thick bushes and old logs."

The halt added hours to the day's march. "It was later than usual," Denny wrote in his journal, "when the army reached the ground this evening, and the men much fatigued prevented the General from having some works of defense immediately erected… The high ground barely sufficient to encamp the army; lines rather contracted."

The 16th camp, however, was not on the St Marys River. The stream was in fact the Wabash, and Kekionga was still 44 miles ahead. There, the Indians had tired of waiting for the Americans. On Friday, October 28, about 1,400 had begun moving southeast.

By November 3, the Indians had reached the trail the army was following. Some 2½ miles from the Americans, where the trail again crossed the river, they had halted. The Shawnee George Ash, whose brother Benjamin would die fighting in Captain Presley Gray's Kentucky militia company, was among them. "When the Indians were within about half a mile of St Clair," he recalled, "the spies came running back to inform us, and we stopped. We concluded to encamp; it was too late, they said, to begin the 'play.' They would defer the sport till the next morning."

THE BATTLE OF THE WABASH

At about 4.00pm on November 3, as snow was falling, Oldham's 260 remaining Kentucky militiamen followed St Clair's Trace to its end at the Wabash River. Ordered to camp beyond the river, they advanced on the Indian trail another 300yds. There, on high, uncleared ground, they camped where a smaller Indian trail led to the north. Between their camp and the site of the main American camp lay a 30ft-deep ravine, through which the Wabash flowed.

About an hour later, as axmen were felling trees to open roads and assembly spaces within the main camp, the army's artillery, wagons, civilians, horses, and oxen reached the area where they would spend the night. The artillery companies occupied their positions behind the guns, which were not, as usual, deployed at the camp's corners and in the center of the camp's long sides. They remained on the trace, at the points where it entered and left the camp. Those in Captain Mahlon Ford's company faced the Kentuckians across the ravine. Those in Captain James Bradford's pointed back down the trace.

The army's wagons stopped halfway along the trace's course through the camp, where their boxes, barrels and bags were unloaded. About 200 civilians, including about 100 women and children, followed. The army's cooks began

This engraving from the *Military Journal of Ebenezer Denny* reproduced Denny's map of the 16th Camp, oriented toward the south. (Author's collection)

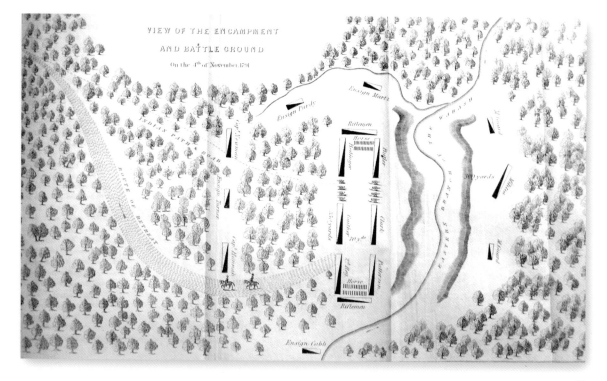

The young warriors at the battle included the Shawnee Tecumseh, who later would become a famous commander in the war against the Americans. This 19th-century engraving, based on a detail of an 1812 sketch by Pierre Le Dru, depicts Tecumseh. (National Anthropological Archives, Smithsonian Institution, BAE GN 00770 06182300)

building long rows of fires behind the camp's front and rear sides. Soon they were baking bread and roasting slaughtered oxen. The army's 400 horses and 130 oxen were turned loose to graze on ground east of the camp,

The two infantry columns, each marching through the woods about 100yds from the trace, halted when they reached the camp. When the officers shouted "carry arms," the order to enter the camp, the right column, which contained Gibson's 2nd Levy Regiment, turned counterclockwise and formed up on the ridge overlooking the ravine along the camp's 375yd-long front side. The left column, which contained Major Jonathan Heart's 2nd Infantry Regiment and Darke's 1st Levy Regiment, turned clockwise and formed the camp's rear side. Because the area of high ground was so small, the distance between the sides was only about 70yds.

When the sun set at 5.43pm the American soldiers were erecting rows of officers' and soldiers' tents behind the camp's sides. Those on the north side of the camp belonged to the 60 riflemen of Faulkner's company and 50 dragoons of Captain Alexander Truman's company.

At the north end of the camp's front side the tents were for the 180 men of Major Thomas Patterson's New Jersey Battalion. The unit had three companies, commanded by Captains Zebulon Pike, William Piatt, and Jonathan Rucastle.

South of the New Jersey men, the 240 officers and soldiers in Major John Clark's Western Pennsylvania Battalion camped. Captain Edward Butler, Richard Butler's brother, commanded one of the unit's four companies. Captains Johann Cribbs and John Guthrie; and Lieutenant George Lukens, whom Sparks had left in command of his unit, led the others.

Below the tents for Clark's men stood those for Ford's artillerymen. To their south the 210 men of the Eastern Pennsylvania Battalion camped. Major Thomas Butler, another Butler brother, commanded the unit. Captain Jacob Slough, Lieutenant-Colonel George Gibson's nephew, led one of the companies. Captains John Smith, William Power, and William Purdy led the three others.

Beyond the cooking fires, another row of tents extended along the rear side of the camp. Those at the north end were for the 235 men of Major Jonathan Heart's 2nd Infantry Regiment. They were in four companies, led by Captains Robert Kirkwood, Patrick Phelon, and Samuel Newman, and by Lieutenant Russell Bissell, Jr, who commanded Shaylor's company in his absence.

South of Heart's soldiers, the 200 men of Major Henry Gaither's Maryland Battalion camped. Captains William Buchanan, Henry Carberry, Benjamin Price, and Swearingen led the unit's four companies. Below the Marylanders stood the tents for Bradford's artillerymen.

South of the artillerymen, in the position once occupied by seven companies of the Virginia and Overmountain Battalions, there now were just 150 men in three companies of the Virginia Battalion. Captain Joseph Darke, Lieutenant-Colonel William Darke's son, Joseph Brock, and Jacob Tipton led the units.

On the camp's south side, the tents were thinner still. In earlier camps, the position had been occupied by Captain Jonathan Snowden's 50-man dragoon company and a 42-man Overmountain Battalion rifle company. Now only Snowden's dragoons were camped between the Virginia and Eastern Pennsylvania Battalions.

The Americans pitched fewer tents than the units' numbers required. St Clair had dispersed about 220 men from the units to six locations beyond the camp. There, 2nd Infantry Regiment Ensign David Cobb, Jr, Captain

Nicholas Hannah, 2nd Regiment Ensign Edward Turner, Captain Samuel Newman, and 2nd Levy Regiment Ensigns William Martz and Hugh Purdy commanded at outposts.

As the Americans encamped, there was much talk of Indians. William Wiseman, a sergeant in Truman's dragoon company, had fought Indians at Dunlap's Station. While scouting on a small prairie that afternoon, he had been "astonished and alarmed by the evidence I saw, by their trail in the grass, of the immediate proximity of a very large force of the enemy."

When Truman ordered his men to lead their horses east of the camp, where they would graze overnight, Wiseman objected. If Indians attacked early the next morning, he said, the horses would be impossible to retrieve. Truman instead ordered the men to gather grass for the horses and to tie them to trees near the dragoons' tents.

At the Indian camp, the Indian commanders met to plan their attack. They agreed on a brilliant, but ambitious, plan, probably proposed by Little Turtle. It would exploit St Clair's dispersal of 260 men across the ravine and another 220 in outposts, and his compression of the remainder of his army into the smallest area into which so many men could fit.

The Indians would attack in a crescent. The Delaware, Miami and Shawnee would form its base. The Mingo, Wyandots and Cherokees would extend forward as its right horn, and the Ottawa, Ojibwe and Potatawatomi as its left. The base of the crescent would strike the militia camp across the Wabash. The horns, racing around the Americans, would overrun the

This winter scene of Ohio woods after a light snow shows the conditions in which the battle was fought. "The day," Jacob Fowler remembered, "was severely cold for the season… My fingers became so benumbed at times that I had to take the bullets in my mouth and load from it." (Author's collection)

outposts. When the horns met, the Indians would occupy positions encircling the main camp, which would offer a compact mass of targets for their muskets.

After the Indian commanders assigned unit placements in the crescent and ultimate line of encirclement, they met with more junior leaders. They, in turn, explained the plan to small-unit leaders and individual warriors. By the time the meetings ended, every Indian warrior understood the plan of attack, what his unit was to do, and what his own role in the battle would be.

Some of the senior commanders addressed the warriors. George Ash remembered Blue Jacket's speech to the Shawnee. "We can do nothing unless assisted by our Great Father above," he said, "I pray now that he will be with us tonight, and ... that tomorrow he will cause the sun to shine out clear upon us, and we will take it as a token of good, and we shall conquer."

By 8.00pm the Americans had eaten breakfast. The drums had beaten "Retreat," and then "Tattoo," the order to remain in tents. As the freezing Americans tried to keep warm, St Clair conferred with his principal officers in his tent near the northeastern corner of the camp. Oldham, worried at the sighting of Indians where his exposed Kentuckians had camped, said that he feared an attack. St Clair ordered Oldham to send out a scouting party to determine whether Indians were near in large numbers. He also directed that all of the Americans should sleep with their weapons ready for immediate use.

St Clair then planned with Major William Ferguson, commander of the artillery and the army's chief engineer, for the construction of a small fortification on the site. There the army would leave a small force to guard the oxen, horses, equipment, and civilians. As soon as it was built, the army would advance to Kekionga by forced march.

Few in either army found it easy to sleep. Some of the Indians tried to steal horses. The Americans, wrapped in thin blankets on frozen ground, heard gunshots every few minutes as their sentries fired at invisible targets. Many thought that Indians would attack the next morning. "The constant discharge of rifles," the surveyor Jacob Fowler wrote, "warned us to prepare for the event." The sound, Wiseman recalled, was "the, to me, unmistakeable noise of the Indians in our vicinity."

Captain Jacob Slough, George Adams, and 23 others volunteered to search for Indians in the dark woods. At 10.00pm they went forward from the Kentucky militia camp on the Indian trail the trace followed. "After passing the militia sentinels," Slough recalled, "I proceeded about a mile up the path... I halted, divided my men into two parties, about thirty or forty yards apart, on each side of the path... ordered them all to lie close down to the ground. We had not long been in this situation before six or seven Indians came along... We fired on them... The Indians ran immediately."

A large party of Indians arrived to search for the Americans, and then a still larger party. Slough's silent men, however, avoided detection. As they retreated in single file on the trail, Slough remembered, "Every fifteen or twenty yards, we heard something moving in the woods, on both sides of the path, but could not see what it was."

By midnight, the Americans had reached safety. Slough then went to report. "I told Colonel Oldham that I was of the same opinion with him that the camp would be attacked in the morning," Slough recalled. He reported what he'd seen to his uncle, and to Richard Butler, but neither awakened St Clair. Slough then retired to his tent and fell asleep. "I never awakened till the firing began on the militia camp," Slough remembered, "I had taken off none of my clothes, expecting what happened."

The battle, 5.30–7.15am

At 5.30am the first sunlight was still more than an hour away. The Indians moved through the woods toward their positions. In the main army camp, the rows of cooking fires began blazing again. Civilians gathered around them as the cooks began to prepare breakfast.

Wiseman, who had spent a sleepless night, could hear in the distance the sounds of the cooks, and also the cries of bears, wolves, and wild turkeys. The animal cries, he concluded, were Indians signaling to one another their positions in the woods. "I conjectured," he remembered, "that the attack was imminent. I therefore roused our company on my own responsibility, and had our horses saddled and bridled, and ordered the men to mount." At last, he awakened Truman, who went to report Wiseman's concern to St Clair.

At about 6.15am St Clair's drummers sounded "Reveille," and then "The Troop," the call for officers and men to take their positions for morning review. Officers' aides, dragoons, and many civilians went to the area east of the camp to search for their horses. St Clair sent Sargent and Denny to the militia camp to get from Oldham any available intelligence about the Indians.

At 6.45am the first sunlight began to illuminate the snowy ground. The Americans had completed the army's morning review. Ordered to keep their weapons with them, they had gathered near the fires where breakfast would be served. Sargent and Denny had returned to the main camp with Oldham, who was to give St Clair a report.

The Indians had formed their crescent about 200yds beyond the outermost militia sentries. The appearance of sunlight was the signal to advance. Captain James Lemon of the Kentucky militia, who had gone beyond the militia camp's farthest guards to scout, saw the Indians first, and was killed. At different points at the edge of the Kentuckians' camp, William Kennan, a scout with the army, and Private Robert Branshaw of the militia, saw in the growing light about 30 Indians moving towards them. "We supposed them," Branshaw recalled, "to be a mere scouting party sent out to gather information about our movements. We did not think that they planned anything more serious than to pick off some of our number and to get a few scalps if they could do so without serious risk. Certain it is, we were not prepared for what took place."

The appearance now of the location of the Kentucky militia camp. The base of the Indian crescent formed along the line occupied by the farm buildings in the background. (Robert Hart)

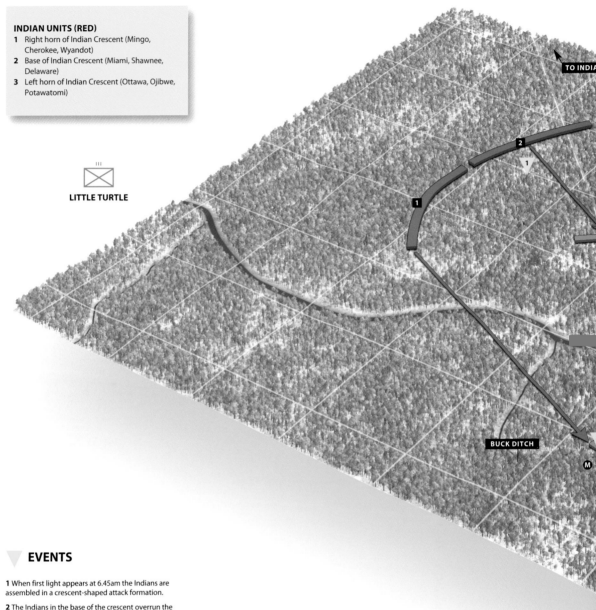

INDIAN UNITS (RED)
1 Right horn of Indian Crescent (Mingo, Cherokee, Wyandot)
2 Base of Indian Crescent (Miami, Shawnee, Delaware)
3 Left horn of Indian Crescent (Ottawa, Ojibwe, Potawatomi)

LITTLE TURTLE

TO INDIAN

BUCK DITCH

EVENTS

1 When first light appears at 6.45am the Indians are assembled in a crescent-shaped attack formation.

2 The Indians in the base of the crescent overrun the 260 Americans in the Kentucky militia camp.

3 The surviving Kentucky militiamen, closely pursued by Indians, flee through the ravine to the main American camp, where they disrupt attempts to form into battle lines by the men of Major Thomas Butler's Eastern Pennsylvania Battalion, Captain Mahlon Ford's artillery company, and Major John Clark's Western Pennsylvania Battalion.

4 The Indians pursuing the militiamen rush into the front line of the main camp. After brief fighting, the Indians retreat.

5 The Indians in the left horn of the crescent overrun the first of the six 40-man American outposts, killing its commander, Ens. David Cobb, Jr.

6 The Indians in the left horn of the crescent overrun Captain Nicholas Hannah's outpost.

7 The Indians in the left horn of the crescent overrun Ens. Edward Turner's outpost, capturing Turner.

8 The Indians in the right horn of the crescent overrun Ens. William Martz's outpost.

9 The Indians in the right horn of the crescent overrun Ens. Hugh Purdy's outpost, killing Purdy.

10 The Indians in the right horn of the crescent overrun Captain Samuel Newman's outpost.

11 By approximately 7.15am the Indians have encircled the American army. Many of the 500 men in the Kentucky militia camp and outposts have been killed or wounded. Most of the others are scattered in the main camp.

THE INDIAN ATTACK

On November 4, 1791, the Indian army attacks the encamped American army at approximately 6.45–7.15am.

ST CLAIR

TO GIRTY'S TOWN

WABASH RIVER

ST CLAIR'S TRACE

TO FORT JEFFERSON

N

AMERICAN UNITS (BLUE)

A Kentucky Militia Companies (Lieutenant-Colonel William Oldham)

B Eastern Pennsylvania Battalion, 2nd US Levy Regiment (Major Thomas Butler)

C Artillery company (Captain Mahlon Ford) (3 x 6-pdr guns)

D Western Pennsylvania Battalion, 2nd US Levy Regiment (Major John Clark)

E New Jersey Battalion, 2nd US Levy Regiment (Major Thomas Patterson)

F Pennsylvania Militia Rifle Company (Captain William Faulkner)

G Dragoon company (Captain Alexander Truman)

H 2nd US Infantry Regiment (Major Jonathan Heart)

I Maryland Battalion, 1st US Levy Regiment (Major Henry Gaither)

J Artillery company (Captain James Bradford) (3 x 3-pdr guns)

K Virginia Battalion, 1st US Levy Regiment (Captain Nicholas Hannah)

L Dragoon company (Captain Jonathan Snowden)

M Outpost (Ens. William Martz)

N Outpost (Ens. Hugh Purdy)

O Outpost (Captain Samuel Newman)

P Outpost (Ens. Edward Turner)

Q Outpost (Captain Nicholas Hannah)

R Outpost (Ens. David Cobb, Jr)

This H. N. Keller engraving from William Dean Howells's 1897 *Stories of Ohio* shows the Kentucky frontiersman William Kennan leaping over a fallen tree in the ravine. (Author's collection)

Kennan and Branshaw fired their rifles. The discharges provoked a massive response. Hundreds of balls flew at them from the woods. Kennan, at 18 already an experienced frontiersman, assumed a prone position on the ground, and began reloading his rifle. He then heard someone shout "Run, Kennan, or you're a dead man."

Hundreds of Indians, visible to the north and south of the militia camp, were racing to surround it. After firing about 50 shots, the Kentuckians fled down into the ravine toward the main American camp. Those who paused to reload died. Many of the Kentuckians neither fired nor ran. The Indians, Branshaw recalled, were screaming "with such appalling effect that I believe some of our men, who might otherwise have escaped, became bewildered, stupefied, and lost." Terrified by the Indians, the newcomers to the west were paralyzed by fear. They died, said the frontiersman Stace McDonough, "like a herd of cattle, without the least attempt to fight, or defend themselves. They were butchered, like so many bullocks in a pen."

Closely pursued by Indians, both Kennan and Branshaw found their path through the ravine already blocked. Fleeing up the Wabash, Kennan escaped a warrior's tomahawk by a prodigious leap over a fallen tree, and Branshaw by killing a pursuer with his knife. Both finally reached the northern end of the main camp.

The shots, and the distant cries of the Indians, which sounded, Sargent remembered, like "an infinitude of horse bells," attracted the attention of those in the main camp. Oldham hurried back toward his men. On the trace between the main camp and the river he fell trying to halt the fleeing Kentuckians.

St Clair's drummers beat "To Arms," the call for men to assume their formations for battle. The generals, colonels, and majors, who would command on horseback, sent aides for their mounts. The captains, lieutenants, and ensigns found their positions in the battle line, and prepared to form their companies.

The fleeing militiamen sped by Ford's guns, trampling down the tents of his artillerymen and of Clark's and Thomas Butler's levies. Some ran through the camp, found horses to the east, and fled down the trace. Others, their units impossible to restore, began wandering through the camp. Still others sought suitable positions to fight. "Thinking I could do quite as well alone as by attaching myself to any company," recalled Branshaw, "I hastened to a tree that looked suitable for my purpose."

Jacob Fowler, who had a similar plan, had no balls for his rifle. He found, however, a wounded Kentucky militiaman with balls to spare. Fowler could have exactly half his supply, the Kentuckian joked, but would have to count how many he took. "It was no time for laughing," Fowler recalled, "but I could hardly resist my impulse to laugh … when they were about to be so plenty as to be had for the picking up by those who should be lucky enough to escape with their lives."

Around the perimeter of the American camp, the officers began forming their men into companies ready for battle. The fleeing militiamen, however, made it difficult for Ford's artillerymen to man their guns, and for Clark's and Thomas Butler's captains to form their units. Then, with the last militiamen to reach the ridge, came screaming Indians.

As Indians overran the area around Ford's guns, the civilians scattered. The men grabbed their rifles and looked for trees as battle positions. The women and children fled to where the wagons had been parked on the trace. "Some," Branshaw remembered "were running to and fro, wringing their hands and shrieking out their terrors; some were standing speechless, like statues of horror... some were kneeling and calling on Heaven for protection; some were sobbing and groaning in each other's arms; and several who had swooned from fright lay as if dead upon the ground." Some of the terrified militiamen and levies sought refuge with the women and children. The women, Sargent wrote, "drove out the skulking militia and fugitives of other corps from under wagons and hiding places by firebrands and the usual weapons of their sex."

As the Indians who had pursued the Kentuckians fought and then scalped around Ford's guns, those in the horns of the Indian crescent raced to surround the American camp. The Ottawa, Ojibwe, and Potatawatomi killed Cobb and his men. The Mingo, Wyandots, and Cherokees overran Martz's and Purdy's outposts. The Americans at Hannah's, Turner's, and Newman's outposts fled back to the camp through a noisy chaos of animals and men. Some tried to find their horses and lead them to the camp, while others sought mounts upon which to flee. Hundreds of horses and oxen, frightened by the shots and screams, stampeded east into deeper woods.

Clark's and Thomas Butler's captains were at last able to organize the men in their levy companies. Musket fire at only a few yards killed some of the Indians around Ford's guns. Bayonets drove the others back. Soon, the surviving Indians fled from the ridge back down into the ravine.

The view now from the ravine looking up at the ridge where St Clair's army was camped. Ford's artillery company was near the location of the white structure to the left of center. (Robert Hart)

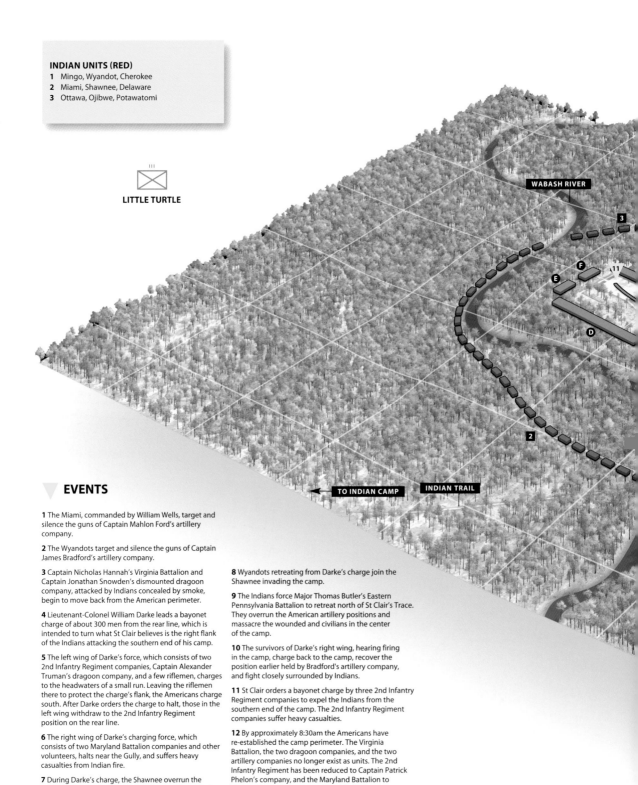

INDIAN UNITS (RED)
1 Mingo, Wyandot, Cherokee
2 Miami, Shawnee, Delaware
3 Ottawa, Ojibwe, Potawatomi

LITTLE TURTLE

WABASH RIVER

TO INDIAN CAMP

INDIAN TRAIL

▼ EVENTS

1 The Miami, commanded by William Wells, target and silence the guns of Captain Mahlon Ford's artillery company.

2 The Wyandots target and silence the guns of Captain James Bradford's artillery company.

3 Captain Nicholas Hannah's Virginia Battalion and Captain Jonathan Snowden's dismounted dragoon company, attacked by Indians concealed by smoke, begin to move back from the American perimeter.

4 Lieutenant-Colonel William Darke leads a bayonet charge of about 300 men from the rear line, which is intended to turn what St Clair believes is the right flank of the Indians attacking the southern end of his camp.

5 The left wing of Darke's force, which consists of two 2nd Infantry Regiment companies, Captain Alexander Truman's dragoon company, and a few riflemen, charges to the headwaters of a small run. Leaving the riflemen there to protect the charge's flank, the Americans charge south. After Darke orders the charge to halt, those in the left wing withdraw to the 2nd Infantry Regiment position on the rear line.

6 The right wing of Darke's charging force, which consists of two Maryland Battalion companies and other volunteers, halts near the Gully, and suffers heavy casualties from Indian fire.

7 During Darke's charge, the Shawnee overrun the positions held by the Virginia Battalion and Snowden's dragoon company.

8 Wyandots retreating from Darke's charge join the Shawnee invading the camp.

9 The Indians force Major Thomas Butler's Eastern Pennsylvania Battalion to retreat north of St Clair's Trace. They overrun the American artillery positions and massacre the wounded and civilians in the center of the camp.

10 The survivors of Darke's right wing, hearing firing in the camp, charge back to the camp, recover the position earlier held by Bradford's artillery company, and fight closely surrounded by Indians.

11 St Clair orders a bayonet charge by three 2nd Infantry Regiment companies to expel the Indians from the southern end of the camp. The 2nd Infantry Regiment companies suffer heavy casualties.

12 By approximately 8:30am the Americans have re-established the camp perimeter. The Virginia Battalion, the two dragoon companies, and the two artillery companies no longer exist as units. The 2nd Infantry Regiment has been reduced to Captain Patrick Phelon's company, and the Maryland Battalion to Captain Henry Carberry's and Captain William Buchanan's companies.

THE AMERICAN CAMP

Between approximately 7.15 and 8.30am the Indians invade the camp, and are attacked by American bayonet charges.

Note: Gridlines are shown at intervals of 100m/109yds

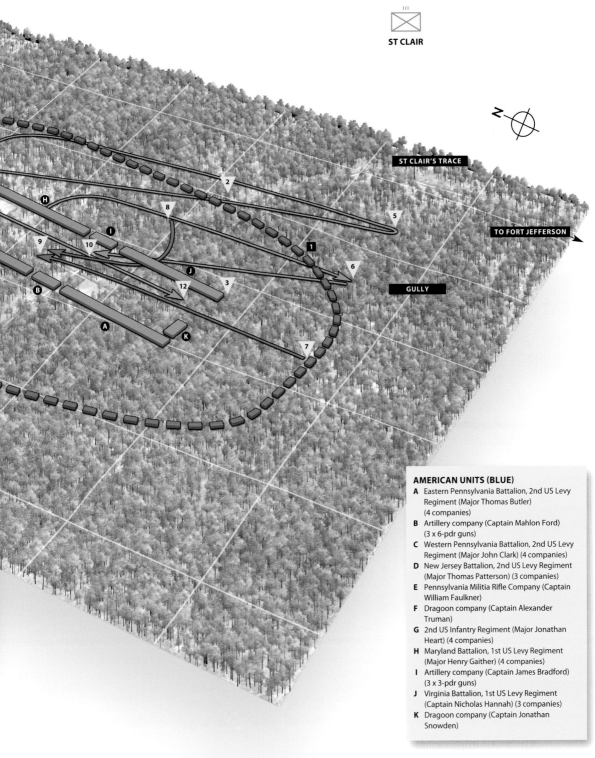

ST CLAIR

ST CLAIR'S TRACE

TO FORT JEFFERSON

GULLY

AMERICAN UNITS (BLUE)
A Eastern Pennsylvania Battalion, 2nd US Levy
Regiment (Major Thomas Butler)
(4 companies)
B Artillery company (Captain Mahlon Ford)
(3 x 6-pdr guns)
C Western Pennsylvania Battalion, 2nd US Levy
Regiment (Major John Clark) (4 companies)
D New Jersey Battalion, 2nd US Levy Regiment
(Major Thomas Patterson) (3 companies)
E Pennsylvania Militia Rifle Company (Captain
William Faulkner)
F Dragoon company (Captain Alexander
Truman)
G 2nd US Infantry Regiment (Major Jonathan
Heart) (4 companies)
H Maryland Battalion, 1st US Levy Regiment
(Major Henry Gaither) (4 companies)
I Artillery company (Captain James Bradford)
(3 x 3-pdr guns)
J Virginia Battalion, 1st US Levy Regiment
(Captain Nicholas Hannah) (3 companies)
K Dragoon company (Captain Jonathan
Snowden)

63

At 7.13am, the sun that Blue Jacket had anticipated rose in a cloudless sky. The Indian commanders had accomplished a feat that few would have thought possible. In less than 30 minutes they had moved 1,400 warriors through enemy positions into precise locations around the main American camp. Almost a quarter of the American army had ceased to be soldiers in units subject to effective command. Half of the American dragoons had no horses. At a distance of 100–150yds from their surrounded enemies, an encircling line of Indians, dispersed to fight six deep, awaited the battle's next stage.

The battle, 7.15–8.30am

As a 25-year-old lieutenant, St Clair had dashed across the Plains of Abraham in 1759, and had been cited for special bravery in one of the greatest victories in British military history. Now, paralyzed by gout, he could not even put on his uniform. He threw over his bedclothes an old black coat, covered his head with a battered black hat, and left his tent. As he tried to mount, two horses were shot from beneath him. A massive infusion of adrenaline then overcame his pain, and he took command on foot.

Richard Butler and Gibson rode back and forth along the front side of the camp, and Darke along the rear. The American majors rode behind their battalions. The captains, lieutenants, and ensigns stood with their men in proper company positions. Musket balls flew through the American camp from all directions. Men who appeared to be American officers attracted them in swarms.

The Americans could see little in the surrounding woods. Small flashes of light, and then clouds of smoke, revealed where Indian muskets had fired. Distant, silent, figures then sped from cover to cover, changing their locations after every shot. "When fairly fixed around us," Denny remembered, "they made no noise but their fire, which they kept up very constant and which seldom failed to tell, although scarcely heard."

All around the camp, the Indians tried to creep forward. In the north, where Faulkner's riflemen watched behind cover, they soon learned the danger of approaching too close. Elsewhere, the Americans could not effectively target the Indians. At intervals, the officers had their men fire musket barrages into the woods. It was, Fowler recalled, "little better than firing at random."

The crews of Ford's and Bradford's guns, at last using their training in battle, fired shots as fast as possible. The noise was audible from 30 miles away. There the 1st Infantry Regiment, returning from pursuing the deserting militiamen, had spent the night at the army's 11th Camp. The faint thunder, Hamtramck and Ziegler knew, was the sound of battle. After quickly striking camp, the unit marched up the trace.

To the Americans at the battle, the deafening roar was the sound of safety. The guns, firing tin canisters filled with balls, poured an immense quantity of munitions into the woods. But the discharges caused few Indian casualties. "Concealed as the enemy were," Sargent wrote," it was almost impossible to discover them and aim the pieces to advantage; but a large quantity of canister and some round shot were, however, thrown among them."

The shot from Ford's guns, aimed at the militia camp, went above the Miamis in the ravine. There the Indians experienced a downpour of wood. Every few seconds, dissolving canisters from the guns sent 56 balls into the tree branches above them. On the rear side of the camp, Bradford's smaller guns were more effective. They sent deadly disks of balls directly into the Wyandots 100yds away. The disks, however, about 4yds in diameter, left most of their 34 balls in the tree trunks of the thick woods.

The Indians, guided by expert advice from British officers on the danger of the American guns, had given careful thought to how to silence them. A company of Miami warriors, led by William Wells, was to concentrate its fire on Ford's artillerymen. A similar Wyandot unit probably targeted Bradford's.

The smoke from the American artillery and musket fire soon created a huge cloud. Blown by a light wind from the northwest, it covered most of the southern area of the American camp like a thick fog. It concealed from the Indians the American artillerymen, and the men in Clark's, Thomas Butler's, Snowden's, Hannah's, and Gaither's units. The barrels of the American guns, however, emitted flames at each discharge.

The Indians sent hundreds of musket balls at the flames. As the unprotected artillery officers and men fell, their rate of fire slowed. Then, to the horror of the Americans, the firing of the guns ceased. "If they would have had a good breastwork to shelter themselves," said Irwin, "all the Indians that was there could not have fazed them."

As silence replaced the roar of the guns, the Indians moved forward into the smoke. The Americans in Clark's and Thomas Butler's battalions were 30ft above the Indians in the ravine. The men in Gaither's, Hannah's, and Snowden's units, however, had no such protection.

The Americans were thinnest at the southeastern corner of the camp. There, Hannah and Snowden had about 200 men. Blinded by the smoke, the Americans there slowly moved back from their positions on the American perimeter, seeking safety in greater distance from the unseen enemy.

When the smoke began to clear, the Americans could see Indians within the camp perimeter. Indian muskets killed from 10yds away, and tomahawks in close combat. The men in Power's Eastern Pennsylvania Battalion company, who now could see Indians behind them, joined in the fighting. With the remaining men of Hannah's and Snowden's units, they drove the Shawnees back.

This detail from a 19th-century engraving, based on a miniature portrait by an unknown artist, shows William Wells, the brother of Captain Samuel Wells of the Kentucky militia. Captured as a boy, he grew to manhood as the Miami Apokonit. In 1791 his wife, Little Turtle's daughter, was captured during Wilkinson's raid on L'Anguille. In 1792 he met his brother at a prisoner exchange. Persuaded to return to Kentucky, he then led a company of American scouts during Wayne's campaign. In 1812 Wells died trying to save Fort Dearborn, in what is now Chicago, where his niece, Samuel Wells's daughter, was the wife of the fort commander. (Chicago Historical Society, ICHi-61498)

THE WABASH RAVINE, NOVEMBER 4, 1791, 7.15AM (pp. 66–67)

At 6.45am, attacking Indians quickly overran the Kentucky militia camp. The surviving militiamen then fled down an Indian trail into the ravine through which the Wabash River flows. Across the river, the militiamen reached the end of St Clair's Trace, which they followed up the other side of the ravine to the ridge on which the American army was encamped. Indians pursuing the militiamen attacked the camp, but were driven back.

This artwork shows the scene a half hour after the first Indian attack. Indians now surround the camp. Those in the foreground are Miami Indians, in positions across the Wabash from the end of St Clair's Trace. Miamis behind trees **(1)** and on the ground **(2)** are firing muskets at American soldiers on the ridge. To their right lies a Kentucky frontiersman **(3)**, who has been overtaken and scalped. Ahead, before the Wabash, and along St Clair's Trace, the bodies of other dead Kentucky militiamen **(4)** can be seen. To their right and left, Miamis **(5)** are returning from their

attack on the camp. On the ridge, the three 6-pdr guns of Captain Mahlon Ford's Company **(6)** have begun firing at the Miamis. The tree branches above and ahead of the Miamis are shaking, as balls from fired American artillery canisters strike them about every ten seconds. To the left of the guns, which are aimed too high to harm the Miamis, are soldiers of Major John Clark's Western Pennsylvania Battalion **(7)**. To the right are those of Major Thomas Butler's Eastern Pennsylvania Battalion **(8)**. In the right foreground is the Miami commander William Wells **(9)**. Captured by the Miami as a boy, Wells was the brother of Captain Samuel Wells, a Kentucky militia commander who survived the Indian attack. Wells is listening to a British officer **(10)**, one of two from the 24th (2nd Warwickshire) Regiment of Foot covertly sent from the Detroit garrison to advise the Indians. The officer, who is wearing the winter coat of an Ojibwe warrior and carrying an Ojibwe war club, is urging him to advance the Miami line closer to the American artillery.

At the northern end of the American camp, their view unobstructed by the smoke, Faulkner's riflemen kept the Indians at a distance. Patterson's and Clark's Battalions on the front line, and the 2nd Infantry Regiment and Maryland Battalion companies on the rear, were also not under heavy attack. To St Clair it appeared that a line of Indians had attacked from the southwest. The left wing of their line had overrun the militia camp and

This photograph of re-enactors firing a 6-pdr gun shows the flames and smoke produced at each discharge. The six American guns could produce about 24 such discharges a minute. (Courtesy of the First Mad River Light Artillery Company and Clark County (Ohio) Park District)

unsuccessfully attacked his front line. The right wing was now threatening to break through the southern part of his rear line. The most effective response, he thought, would be a charge that would turn the Indians' right flank. "Finding no great effect from the fire, and confusion beginning to spread," St Clair wrote, "it became necessary to try what could be done with the bayonet. Lieutenant-Colonel Darke was accordingly ordered to make a charge with part of the second line, and to turn the flank of the enemy."

Darke assembled about 300 men in a line centered between the 2nd Infantry Regiment and Maryland Battalion positions. On its left, Heart led Newman's and Shaylor's 2nd Regiment companies and Truman's dragoons. On its right, Darke led Swearingen's and Price's Maryland Battalion companies. Small groups of riflemen, gathered from the surviving militiamen and civilians, would advance at the ends to protect the line's flanks. Leaving four companies to defend an area of the rear line that had been held by eight, they would charge forward from the rear line, and then wheel clockwise to the south, driving the Indians before them.

The American officers shouted "Fix bayonets," and then "Advance arms." The men went forward as they had been trained, walking in 2ft paces in the "common step," at a rate of 72 paces a minute. Then, at the command "Charge bayonets," they moved in the "quick step," at a rate of 120 paces a minute.

As the Americans approached, the Indians rose from the ground like flushed birds. Those directly ahead of the charge fell back, maintaining a distance of about 50yds. Others fled left and right to positions at a similar distance. "The Indians," Denny observed, "seemed not to fear anything we could do. They could skip out of the reach of the bayonet and return as they pleased."

As the Indians fell back before the American bayonets, the dragoons in Truman's company pursued them with sabres at the extreme left of the charge. Hoping to begin a rout of the Indians, they soon lost contact with the 2nd Infantry Regiment companies. The Indians, after firing at the dragoons and retreating, raced to surround them. Soon, balls from every direction were killing the encircled American horsemen. Only 13 survived, including Truman and William Wiseman.

Wiseman was with the dragoon commander. "I could see no one but the captain," he recalled, "it seemed we were entirely cut off." Then Truman, as he rode his horse in a clockwise circle to examine the surrounding woods, was hit by balls in his left wrist and left hip. As Wiseman led him back to the camp, another ball severed two fingers of his left hand. "As we entered the camp," Wiseman remembered, "I perceived some twenty or thirty of our horses without their riders, but all bridled and saddled, had run into the camp, and were congregated under an oak tree near the lines."

THE CENTER OF THE AMERICAN CAMP, NOVEMBER 4, 1791, 8.15AM (pp. 70–71)

After an hour and a half of battle the Americans tried to drive the Indians from their rear line in a wheeling charge to the right led by Lieutenant-Colonel William Darke. As the Americans charged, Shawnee and then Wyandot Indians broke through the weakly held southeastern corner of the American perimeter. After racing into the interior of the American camp, they massacred the wounded and civilians and looted the army's supplies.

This artwork shows three companies of 2nd Infantry Regiment soldiers charging to expel them. The figures in the foreground are in the center of the American camp, where the army's wagons and supplies were located, and where the women, children, and wounded had been sent to what was believed to be an area of safety. On the left stands a US Army supply wagon (1), from which boxes, kegs, and bags have been unloaded. A well-dressed boy near the wagon, the son of

an American officer, has been killed and scalped (2). Three dead women (3) lie nearby. A Shawnee warrior (4) is carrying a keg of powder back to the Indian line, as another (5) scalps a wounded Virginia Battalion soldier (6). The cautious Shawnee commander Black Hoof (7) is shouting at the warriors to retreat as the charging Americans advance toward the area. As a Shawnee warrior (8) flees, others (9) continue firing at the advancing Americans. In the distance 2nd Infantry Regiment Major Jonathan Heart (10), who had left his son in the center of the American camp, has been hit by a musket ball while leading the American charge. To his left, the 2nd Infantry companies of Captain Samuel Newman (11), who had also left his son there, and to his right, those of Captain Robert Kirkwood (12), the "Blue Hen of Delaware," continue to advance, though Newman and Kirkwood have been killed.

After the other Americans had advanced about 400yds around trees and over logs, their line had lost its order. When the men on the extreme right reached a gully left by the flow of Buck Ditch, Darke, who could no longer see any fleeing Indians, halted the charge. The Indians then began to target the stationary Americans. Soon, Swearingen and Price were dead.

The Americans then heard shouting and firing from the northwest. "I judged by the shouting and firing," Fowler said, "that the Indians behind us had closed up the gap we had made in charging." Darke ordered the American infantrymen to return to the camp. Heart's soldiers marched back in good order. Moving in quick step as men fell around them, they were soon back at the position from which they had charged.

The scattered Maryland levies were harder to organize. The civilian horsemaster Benjamin Van Cleve, in a position overlooking the gully, was the farthest man on their right. The Indians fleeing the bayonets, he recalled, "ran to the right, where there was a small ravine filled with logs. I bent my course after them, and on looking round found I was with only seven or eight men, the others having kept straight forward and halted about thirty yards off. We halted also, and being so near where the savages lay concealed, the second fire from them left me standing alone... I fired away all my ammunition... then looked for the party near me, and saw them retreating and half way back to the lines. I followed them, running my best, and was soon in."

As Darke was organizing his charge, many Shawnee, discouraged at the casualties they had suffered fighting in the smoke, had begun leaving the field. Black Fish, George Ash recalled, then had stopped them. "In a voice of thunder," Ash remembered, the Shawnee commander demanded to know who had ordered the retreat. "You who are like-minded," he shouted, "follow me."

As Darke's men had advanced, the Shawnee had attacked again. Wyandots and Mingos fleeing the American bayonets had joined them. After overpowering the remaining defenders in Hannah's and Snowden's units, they had raced forward into the American camp. The Eastern Pennsylvania Battalion, under attack from three sides, had fallen back to the area around

LEFT
This sculpture in Fort Recovery by Phil Wood depicts "Red-headed Nance." The wife of Private Horace Miller of the 1st Infantry Regiment, she was one of the army's cooks. When Indians invaded the camp, she fought them with a frying pan while holding her baby. During the army's retreat, she had to abandon the baby, whom she no longer had the strength to carry. (Robert Hart)

RIGHT
Five years before he became US president, Theodore Roosevelt wrote the first detailed account of the battle. This engraving by Rufus F. Zogbaum illustrated Roosevelt's 1896 *St Clair's Defeat*, which appeared in *Harper's Magazine*. (Photograph Courtesy of *Harper's Magazine*)

Ford's guns. The screaming Indians reached the center of the camp, where the army's wagons and supplies had been left. There, where the women and children had sought safety, the American wounded were being treated. "The attack," George Ash recalled, "was most impetuous, and the carnage for a few minutes shocking. Many of the Indians threw away their guns, leaping in among the Americans, and did the butchery with the tomahawks."

When Darke's Maryland levies returned to the camp they found a scene of indescribable chaos. Richard Butler, who had tried to halt the American flight north, had been wounded. Thomas Butler was trying to organize the Americans into a new line, anchored on the right by Clark's southernmost company. There were, Darke recalled, "scalped, I suppose, a hundred men or more."

North of the trace, a crowd of soldiers without officers or weapons had gathered to watch the horror around the American wagons. Some Indians were killing and scalping the women and children. Others were throwing wounded men into the cooking fires. Still others were pillaging the supplies for gunpowder.

Branshaw, his wrist shattered by a musket ball, had left his tree. As he walked to the center of the camp to get medical aid, he met "pale, frightened men running in all directions… When I came within sight of the spot where the women and children had been collected, I beheld a large body of Indians busy at their work of slaughter." Branshaw found a horse in the area east of the camp and fled down the trace.

Many of Darke's men ran north toward safety. With those who remained, he recovered the area around Bradford's guns. Wyandots who had followed Darke's return to the camp then attacked his diminished force from behind. Soon, Fowler said, "there were about thirty men of Colonel Darke's command left standing, the rest being all shot down and lying around us." Fowler and the others then fought surrounded. Darke saw the civilian horsemaster John Hamilton kill an Indian with his tomahawk. Fowler saw Darke behead another with his sword.

St Clair and Heart assembled a force to recover the southern end of the camp. The remains of Newman's and Shaylor's units, and the men in Kirkwood's 2nd Infantry Regiment company, fixed their bayonets and charged south. Men from Clark's and Thomas Butler's battalions joined them.

Led by Heart and Newman, who had left their 12- and 11-year-old sons in the area the Indians had overrun, the Americans drove the Indians from the camp. They suffered, however, heavy casualties. By the end of the charge, Heart, Newman, Kirkwood, and most of the other 2nd Infantry Regiment officers were dead.

The battle, 8.30–9.45am

By 8.30am St Clair had reestablished his perimeter. Richard Butler, his arm in a sling, returned to take command of the front line. Darke, with a musket ball in one leg, insisted on retaining command of the rear. Thomas Butler, whose falling horse had broken his leg, continued to lead his men. Some of the officers had even begun firing Ford's and Bradford's guns again.

The Indians had fled from the charging bayonets back to their original line. The American army, however, now had only a fraction of its former strength. Within the camp there were hundreds of wounded men who could no longer fight, and hundreds of unwounded who were too demoralized to try.

North of St Clair's Trace, Faulkner's company, Patterson's three New Jersey Battalion companies, and Clark's four Western Pennsylvania Battalion companies remained intact. The rear line, however, had now lost five of its eight companies. The 2nd Infantry Regiment had been reduced to Phelon's company. Gaither's Battalion had only Carberry's and Buchanan's companies.

Elsewhere, remnants of units fighting with surviving officers and leaderless men fighting for their lives defended the American perimeter. Two hours before, more than 400 officers and men had defended the portion south of the trace. Now there were about 150. Hannah, who no longer had a battalion to command, was operating one of Bradford's guns. Snowden was wounded, and most of his 50 dragoons dead. Thomas Butler's battalion, diminished by casualties, had the only remaining intact companies.

The Indians again commenced their pattern of attack. Musket fire targeted the artillery. Indians crept forward from tree to log, firing, reloading, and then advancing again. The Shawnee, Wyandots, and Mingos, who had suffered significant casualties, advanced cautiously. The Miami and Delaware facing Thomas Butler's line, however, had not participated in the fighting in the smoke or in Black Fish's invasion of the American camp. They advanced rapidly. Soon they were approaching the top of the ridge. Richard Butler fell, mortally wounded. Thomas Butler's line threatened to collapse.

St Clair sent the last intact 2nd Infantry Regiment unit, Phelon's company, to reinforce the Eastern Pennsylvanians. Phelon and his men, and Thomas Butler and his, drove the Miami and Delaware back down into the ravine. They then charged after the Indians into devastating musket fire. A few of the Americans made it across the Wabash. Phelon and most of the men in his company were killed. Thomas Butler, wounded in his other leg, was carried back to safety.

The fighting then stopped. Many Indians had fallen. Others had exhausted their powder. As the Indian commanders considered withdrawal, St Clair briefly concluded that the Americans, at great cost, had prevailed. St Clair, Denny recalled, asked him "how long the battle had lasted … and seemed pleased in the idea of repelling the savages and keeping the ground." The Indian commanders, however, decided to continue the attack. After 15 minutes, the Indians began to advance again. Three hours before, St Clair had had too many men to fit into his camp. He now, he believed, had too few to defend its perimeter. When he ordered a retreat to the northern part of the camp, some of his officers objected. William Wiseman overheard Darke arguing with the American commander, and telling him that he was "bringing us all together to be shot down like a flock of partridges."

As word spread that the southern part of the camp would have to be abandoned, Richard Butler was resting on his mattress, which had been propped against a tree. Thomas Butler, with both legs now useless, and Edward Butler, who was unwounded, were with him. The mortally wounded general, a witness recalled, "begged of those who were with him not to remain longer on his account. He gave his ring, sword and watch to one of the gentlemen, and in exchange requested a loaded pistol that he might as long as possible defend himself, which was accordingly cocked and put into his hand."

The Americans spiked their artillery, evacuated the mobile wounded, and retired north. There Patterson's New Jersey Battalion, Faulkner's company, and Carberry's and Buchanan's companies defended what was left of the original American perimeter. To complete a new perimeter, St Clair ordered Clark's Western Pennsylvania Battalion to turn 90 degrees and face south.

The Indians then closed in around the Americans, who were confined to an area of about 3 acres. The surviving officers, most of whom were wounded, could no longer persuade their men to obey orders. The men, Fowler said, "appeared stupefied and bewildered." Some silently wrapped themselves in blankets to await their fate in warmth. Others had a late breakfast. Some gathered in a crowd, Darke said, "like a mob at a fair."

Some Indians fired muskets into the mass of Americans. Others, their powder exhausted, began to shoot arrows. "As our lines were deserted," Denny wrote, "the Indians contracted theirs... Exposed to a cross fire, men and officers were seen falling in every direction; the distress too of the wounded made the scene such as can scarcely be conceived."

By 9.30am, half of the 1,900 Americans on the field were dead or wounded. St Clair realized that the army would have to flee. The thought of leaving the immobile wounded to the Indians was so bitter that some, like Clark, opposed retreat. St Clair, however, was left with no other choice. "A few minutes longer," Denny wrote, "and a retreat would have been impracticable. Delay was death; no preparation could be made; numbers of brave men must be left a sacrifice; there was no alternative."

St Clair quickly devised a plan of escape. Faulkner's, Patterson's, and Clark's men would hold their positions. The men defending the remainder of the perimeter would charge east, and feint a clockwise turning. Protected by Clark's battalion, which would serve as a rearguard, the Americans would retreat through the opening left by the charge. Adams would lead them on a wide clockwise turn around the Indians, and reach the trace about a mile southeast of the camp.

St Clair ordered Darke to lead the charge. The men upon whom the army's fate would depend, however, were from units that no longer existed. Few of the captains and lieutenants who had led them remained. In the 2nd Infantry Regiment, all but Lieutenant Russell Bissell, Jr, were dead or wounded; in the 1st Levy Regiment, all but Captains Nicholas Hannah, Joseph Brock, and Henry Carberry; in the Eastern Pennsylvania Battalion, all but Captain William Power.

Darke and his officers ordered the men to assemble for another charge. Drums and commands, then threats and pleas, went unanswered. No one responded.

Carberry had begun his military career in 1776 as a cadet at the battle of Long Island. There almost every man in his Maryland company had died in bayonet charges that had allowed Washington's trapped army to retreat and avoided an early end to the American Revolution. The Maryland captain now saved what was left of the American army. "With great presence of mind," an officer wrote, Carberry began shouting to the soldiers the purpose of the charge, to open a way of escape. "The men" the officer recalled, "instantly fixed bayonets, and ... broke through the Indians like a torrent."

George Adams then ran through the camp, yelling, "Boys let us make for the trace." Kentucky militia sergeant Garret Burns was fighting with Clark's Western Pennsylvania Battalion. Clark, Burns remembered, tried to keep the army's rearguard in order. He shouted, "'Fill up the ranks! Fill up the ranks!' until it was found that we had no men to fill the ranks."

The flight then began. Every American who could run, walk, or stumble went forward into the opening, many carrying wounded relatives or friends on their backs. Behind them, Fowler recalled, "the freshly scalped heads were reeking with smoke, and in the heavy morning frost looked like so many pumpkins through a cornfield in December."

THE AMERICAN RETREAT

At about 9.45pm, St Clair, with eight holes in his coat left by musket balls, left the field with the last of the army. Some 20 miles down the trace, the men of the 1st Infantry Regiment were marching north. They met fleeing militiamen, who told them that Indians were destroying the army. Hamtramck, after sending a detachment forward to get more information, retreated to secure Fort Jefferson.

Adams led the Americans in a wide semicircle around the Indians. When they reached the trace, however, he was unable to persuade them to pause. Down the trace, the strongest and swiftest fled. "The stoutest and most active," Denny wrote, "now took the lead and those who were foremost in

LEFT
In 1792 an escaped Indian captive told Captain Edward Butler that Richard Butler was still alive. Edward Butler then traveled to Detroit, and learned that soon after the Americans had fled an Indian had killed his brother with a tomahawk. When Wayne's army reached the battlefield in 1793 he found his brother's remains near the tree where he had been left. Richard Butler's death caused grief among the Seneca, who had rejected a request to send warriors to join St Clair's army. "I have lost," said the Seneca chief Big Tree (Kiandogewa), "a very dear friend, the friend of my heart." After considering suicide, and waging a personal campaign of vengeance against the Ohio Indians, Big Tree joined Wayne's army in 1793. When it briefly appeared in early 1794 that Wayne's campaign would end without further bloodshed, Big Tree killed himself. (Robert Hart)

RIGHT
This Rufus F. Zogbaum engraving from Roosevelt's *St Clair's Defeat* shows the surrounded remnant of the American army. (Photograph Courtesy of Harper's Magazine)

THE LAST CHARGE, NOVEMBER 4, 1791, 9.30AM (pp. 78–79)

After almost three hours of battle, the Americans, stunned by the failure of repeated bayonet charges and Indian infliction of massive casualties, have retreated into an area of about 3 acres at the northern end of the camp. There, where Indian musket balls and arrows are killing more Americans every minute, many have lost the will to continue fighting. After 15 minutes of slaughter in the confined area, the few surviving American officers have realized that the entire army will be lost unless it now flees from the field.

The figures in the foreground are near the northern end of the rear line. The area, originally occupied by a company of the 2nd Infantry Regiment, is now defended by soldiers left from shattered units. In the distance, Ojibwe Indians occupy positions opposite them. American officers are desperately trying to persuade the demoralized soldiers to form a line to charge the Ojibwe with bayonets. Captain Henry Carberry of the Maryland

Battalion (1) is shouting to the soldiers that this charge is to open a path through the Indians by which the army can retreat. Major Thomas Butler (2), who has broken bones in both legs, cannot walk. One of his Eastern Pennsylvania Battalion soldiers (3) will carry him on the path opened by the charge. A Virginia Battalion soldier, who has lost his cheap levy-issue hat and put on a militiaman's (4), is firing at the Indians as another, who has found a warm woolen cap, watches (5). A Maryland Battalion soldier (6), who has wrapped himself in a blanket, sits silently awaiting the end. Three 2nd Infantry Regiment soldiers have begun to form the line (7) as a Maryland Battalion soldier attaches his bayonet to join them (8). Two other 2nd Infantry Regiment soldiers – (9) and (10) – are listening to Carberry and deciding whether or not to join the charge. In the distance the emboldened Ojibwe (11) are firing muskets at the Americans. One (12), his powder exhausted, is using a bow.

breaking the enemy's line were soon left behind." St Clair, mounted on a horse "that could not be pricked out of a walk," moved forward to the head of the retreating column, which grew ever longer as the strong outdistanced the weak. His path through the slushy snow was marked by discarded weapons and equipment. "The road," St Clair remembered, "for miles was covered with firelocks, cartridge boxes and regimentals."

Fowler, after seeing his cousin Captain William Piatt of the New Jersey Battalion fall, raced ahead. "Being uncommonly active in those days," he recalled, "I soon got from the rear to front of the troops, although I had great trouble to avoid the bayonets which the men had thrown off in their retreat."

Many of the Americans tried to find horses for those who could not walk. A Western Pennsylvania Battalion soldier found one for Thomas Butler. Kennan found another for Kentucky militia Captain George Madison, who was wounded in a leg.

Some lost their way in the woods. Private Stephen Littell of the New Jersey Battalion wandered back to the battlefield. The Indians were gone, pursuing the retreating army. The wounded men and women who were still there begged him to kill them before the Indians returned.

At the army's rear, Clark's men briefly delayed the Indian pursuit. Soon, however, Clark was wounded, and the rearguard collapsed. Edward Butler, the only surviving Western Pennsylvania Battalion captain, fled with the survivors. The Indians pursued the Western Pennsylvanians to the rear of the retreating American column. There they killed the weak, the slow, and the burdened. After taking scalps, they moved on for more.

The flight then became a race, in which the Americans competed against one another. "I took the cramp violently in my thighs," Van Cleve remembered, "and could scarcely walk until I got within about a hundred yards of the rear, where the Indians were tomahawking the old and wounded men… I threw the shoes off my feet, and the coolness of the ground seemed to revive me. I again began a trot and… got before a half a dozen persons. I thought it would occupy some time for the enemy to massacre them, before my turn would come."

The Americans who fled too slowly did not survive. Desperate to outpace their pursuers, even the bravest abandoned their burdens when they found themselves near the end of the American column. When a wounded man on Kennan's back refused to release his grip, Kennan cut off his fingers. When an army cook who had fought the Indians in the center of the army camp could carry her baby no longer, the woman, known as "Red-headed Nance," left the baby beside the trace.

LEFT
On the high ground in the distance, 63-year-old Private Michael Hare and others in the Western Pennsylvania Battalion tried to hold back the Indians pursuing the army. Hare, wounded, scalped, and left for dead, ultimately made his way back to Fort Washington. He then survived until 1843, to die at the age of 115. His extraordinary age is known because he owned a life estate in land in Ireland. (Robert Hart)

RIGHT
Robert Benham, who was wounded at the battle, and his nephew Benjamin Van Cleve, were civilian horsemasters who survived the retreat. 12 years before, Benham and another man had been the only American survivors of the battle of the Licking River. Benham, wounded in both legs, and his companion, wounded in both arms, together managed to survive for 19 days on the battlefield before being rescued. In 1792 Benham would begin operating the first regular ferry across the Ohio at Cincinnati. In 1796 Van Cleve would be one of the first settlers of Dayton, Ohio. In this 1796 log cabin in Dayton, he taught at a school for the new settlement's children. (Jonathan Reed Winkler)

The American retreat, November 4–8, 1791

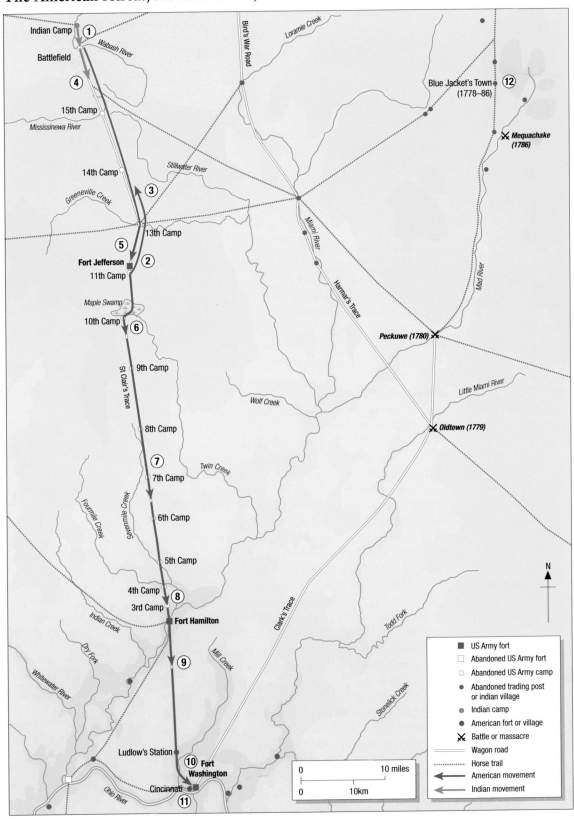

Indian Camp
① ②
Wabash River

Battlefield

④

15th Camp
Mississinewa River

14th Camp

Greeneville Creek

③

13th Camp

⑤

Fort Jefferson
11th Camp

②

Maple Swamp

10th Camp

⑥

St Clair's Trace

9th Camp

8th Camp

⑦

7th Camp

Twin Creek

6th Camp

Fourmile Creek

5th Camp

4th Camp
3rd Camp

⑧

Fort Hamilton

Indian Creek

⑨

Mill Creek

Dry Fork

Whitewater River

Ludlow's Station

⑩ Fort Washington

Cincinnati

⑪

Ohio River

Bird's War Road
Loramie Creek

Blue Jacket's Town
(1778–86)

⑫

Mequachake
(1786)

Stillwater River

Miami River

Harmar's Trace

Mad River

Peckuwe (1780) ✕

Little Miami River

Wolf Creek

Oldtown (1779) ✕

Clark's Trace

Todd Fork

Stonelick Creek

N

■	US Army fort
□	Abandoned US Army fort
○	Abandoned US Army camp
●	Abandoned trading post or indian village
●	Indian camp
●	American fort or village
✕	Battle or massacre
═══	Wagon road
⋯⋯	Horse trail
◀━	American movement
◀━	Indian movement

0   10 miles
0   10km

1 At 6.45am on November 4 the Indians attacked the American 16th Camp.
2 At about 7.15am the 1st Infantry Regiment, camped at the site of the army's 11th Camp, heard artillery fire from the battlefield. The unit advanced north on St Clair's Trace.
3 At about 10.30am on November 4 the 1st Infantry Regiment met Americans who had fled from the battlefield, and returned to Fort Jefferson.
4 At about 10.30am on November 4 the Indians ceased their pursuit of the retreating Americans and returned to the battlefield.
5 At about 7.00pm on November 4 the head of the retreating American column reached Fort Jefferson. At about 10.00pm the Americans left the immobile wounded at the fort and marched toward an advancing food convoy.
6 At about 7.00am on November 5 the Americans stopped and slept in this area. At about 9.00am the advancing food convoy reached them. At 1.00pm the Americans resumed the retreat.

7 At about 9.00pm on November 5 the Americans stopped in this area between the army's 7th and 6th camps and slept.
8 At 9.00am on November 6 the Americans on horseback reached Fort Hamilton. American survivors arrived at the fort all day.
9 At noon on November 7 the Americans resumed the retreat. After marching 8 miles, they stopped in this area.
10 At noon on November 8, St Clair reached Fort Washington. American survivors arrived at the fort throughout the day.
11 Although ordered to camp on a site north of Fort Washington, the American soldiers sought shelter and liquor in the cabins and taverns of Cincinnati.
12 Blue Jacket's Town and other Indian villages between the Miami and Mad Rivers had been destroyed in Logan's 1786 campaign.

After pursuing the Americans for about 4 miles, the Indians returned to the ground the army had abandoned. There, as Littell watched from beneath a fallen tree branch, the Indian commanders divided the spoils. The Delaware chief Big Cat got a lavish share of American equipment to carry back to his village on the Auglaize River. "We then," his adopted son John Brickell remembered, "found ourselves a rich people."

The Indian warriors passed the afternoon feasting on the American food, and torturing the American captives to death. By 6.01pm, when the last daylight left the sky, they had returned to their camp. Concealed by the dark, Littell fled down the ice-covered trace.

An hour later, the head of the American column reached Fort Jefferson. The tiny fort, which offered little protection, also had no food. Shaylor's garrison was on half rations. It was still awaiting the fifth packhorse convoy, which was known to be proceeding from Fort Hamilton, 45 miles away.

St Clair convened a council of his surviving officers. All agreed that the army must leave the immobile wounded with Shaylor's garrison at the fort, and continue the retreat toward the convoy. At 10.00pm, hundreds of men, who already had fled 29 miles from the battlefield, set out down the trace again.

Behind them, they left a scene of misery. Branshaw, who remained, wrote, "Nothing was heard that night but sounds of lamentation and woe. Subsequently my arm was amputated." Darke stayed for a time with his mortally wounded son, Captain Joseph Darke. He then rode south to join the retreat, one of the few unaffected by the cold. "My thigh," he recalled, "was… swelled near as large as my body and so hot I could feel the warmth with my hand two feet off of it."

Those who stumbled south carried their misery with them. In nine hours, they advanced 7 miles. By dawn, they had made their way through Maple Swamp. Unable to go farther, they collapsed beside the trace and slept.

At 9.00am on November 5 the advancing packhorse convoy awakened the sleeping Americans, who then ate double rations. St Clair sent 50 soldiers of the 1st Infantry Regiment back to Fort Jefferson with the convoy. At 1.00pm the army resumed its dreary march. After eight more hours the Americans stopped on the trace to sleep between the sites of their 7th and 6th Camps.

On November 6, St Clair and the others on horseback reached Fort Hamilton at 9.00am. Those on foot reached the fort before dark. After a long night's sleep, they set out again at noon on November 7, but advanced only 8 miles. As

On December 1, 1791, Lieutenant Russell Bissell, Jr, the senior 2nd Infantry Regiment officer to survive the battle, prepared at Fort Washington this roster of the unit's fallen and remaining officers and men. (Courtesy of the Ohio Historical Society)

stragglers continued to reach Fort Jefferson, including one with a tomahawk embedded in his skull, St Clair arrived at Fort Washington on November 8 at about noon. By dark, several hundred freezing, exhausted, and demoralized men, many of them wounded, had reached the end of their 97-mile flight from the battlefield.

The appearance of what had been an army shocked the officers at Fort Washington, including 18-year-old Ensign William Henry Harrison. The wounded were taken to the fort. The others, who had nothing but the clothes on their backs, were told to camp on the frozen ground north of the fort and await further orders.

Cincinnati, however, had taverns and warm cabins. The following day, Sargent wrote in his journal, "Every house in this town is filled with drunken soldiers and there seems one continued scene of confusion." The liquor, however, was soon exhausted. Harrison and other officers bought with their own funds warm coats and blankets for the men. Order was restored. "Great excesses," Sargent wrote in his journal, "were committed in the town." But St Clair made no attempt to punish the soldiers. "Their situation," Sargent said, "was truly distressing, and could only be justly conceived of by experiencing it."

By November 11, those who could were leaving Fort Washington as quickly as possible. As some boarded keelboats to travel up the Ohio, and others crossed the river to begin walking to Lexington, Sparks, Piamingo, and the Chickasaws returned from their scouting expedition. After learning of the battle from a prisoner, they had hurried back, bringing five Indian scalps, and information that would have been invaluable two weeks before.

St Clair himself had a final duty. In his cabin in the southwestern corner of Fort Washington he worked on a report of what had happened for

Washington and Knox. As he labored, others tried to calculate the numbers of American dead and wounded. The exact numbers would never be known. About 700 American officers and soldiers probably fell or died from their wounds. Another 300 were likely wounded, but survived. More than 100 civilians were probably killed, and another 50 wounded. The American casualties, however, may have been much higher. Exact numbers are known only for the 2nd Infantry Regiment. Of the ten officers present at the battle, three ultimately reached Fort Washington, including two without wounds. Of the unit's 224 men at the battle, 84 survived, including 30 who were unwounded. Indian casualties will never be known. All that is certain is that they were only a fraction of the American losses. The numbers of Indian dead and likely wounded were about a tenth of those of the Americans.

On November 18 St Clair concluded his report. "I have now, sir," he ended, "finished my melancholy tale." Sargent wrote in his journal that evening, "Piamingo had his audience of leave from the General this day, and condoled him on the misfortunes of the campaign... He recommended strongly to the General to fight the Indians in their own way from behind logs and trees, and to be continually changing the ground in time of action."

The following day, Denny, who was to carry St Clair's report to Philadelphia, boarded a keelboat for the first stage of his long journey. He reached his destination on December 19. There, after delivering St Clair's report to Knox, he was told that he would meet with President Washington the following morning. That night he wrote in his journal, "Since I left Fort Washington, have endeavored to banish from my mind, as much as possible, every idea of the slaughter and defeat of the army; to talk at all on the subject is an unpleasant task to me, but there are certain persons to whom I must make a full communication."

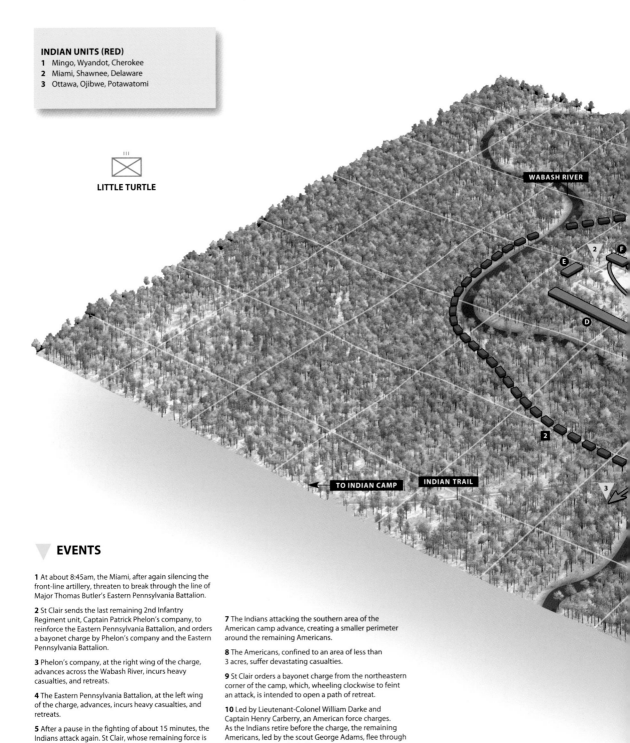

LITTLE TURTLE

WABASH RIVER

TO INDIAN CAMP

INDIAN TRAIL

EVENTS

1 At about 8:45am, the Miami, after again silencing the front-line artillery, threaten to break through the line of Major Thomas Butler's Eastern Pennsylvania Battalion.

2 St Clair sends the last remaining 2nd Infantry Regiment unit, Captain Patrick Phelon's company, to reinforce the Eastern Pennsylvania Battalion, and orders a bayonet charge by Phelon's company and the Eastern Pennsylvania Battalion.

3 Phelon's company, at the right wing of the charge, advances across the Wabash River, incurs heavy casualties, and retreats.

4 The Eastern Pennsylvania Battalion, at the left wing of the charge, advances, incurs heavy casualties, and retreats.

5 After a pause in the fighting of about 15 minutes, the Indians attack again. St Clair, whose remaining force is inadequate to defend the camp perimeter, orders the Americans to spike their artillery and abandon the southern two-thirds of the camp.

6 Major John Clark's Western Pennsylvania Battalion turns 90 degrees to form the southern face of a new American defensive perimeter.

7 The Indians attacking the southern area of the American camp advance, creating a smaller perimeter around the remaining Americans.

8 The Americans, confined to an area of less than 3 acres, suffer devastating casualties.

9 St Clair orders a bayonet charge from the northeastern corner of the camp, which, wheeling clockwise to feint an attack, is intended to open a path of retreat.

10 Led by Lieutenant-Colonel William Darke and Captain Henry Carberry, an American force charges. As the Indians retire before the charge, the remaining Americans, led by the scout George Adams, flee through the gap opened in the Indian perimeter.

11 The Western Pennsylvania Battalion, acting as rearguard, tries to protect the Americans as they flee along a clockwise route of retreat more than a mile to St Clair's Trace. The Indians overrun the rearguard and pursue the routed Americans.

THE AMERICAN COLLAPSE

The Americans are forced to abandon their perimeter and retreat.

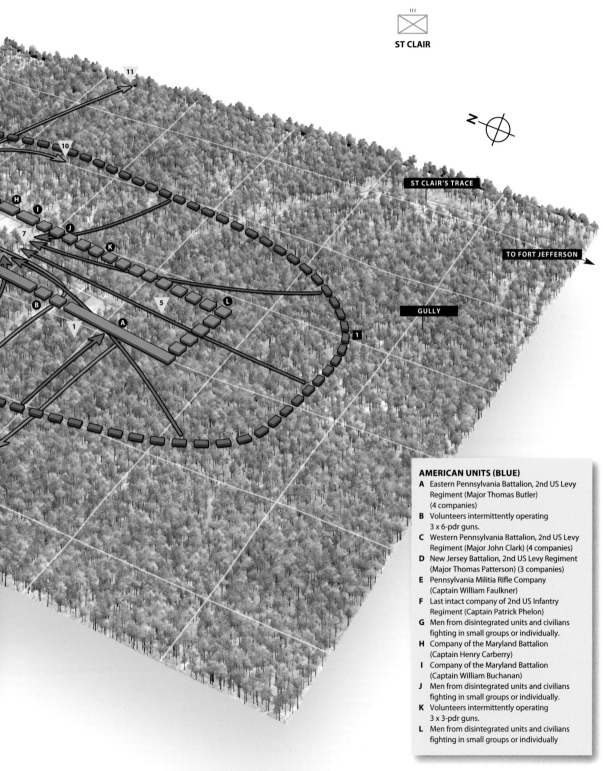

ST CLAIR

N

ST CLAIR'S TRACE

11

10

H

I

7

J

K

TO FORT JEFFERSON

B

5

L

A

1

GULLY

1

AMERICAN UNITS (BLUE)

A Eastern Pennsylvania Battalion, 2nd US Levy Regiment (Major Thomas Butler) (4 companies)

B Volunteers intermittently operating 3 x 6-pdr guns.

C Western Pennsylvania Battalion, 2nd US Levy Regiment (Major John Clark) (4 companies)

D New Jersey Battalion, 2nd US Levy Regiment (Major Thomas Patterson) (3 companies)

E Pennsylvania Militia Rifle Company (Captain William Faulkner)

F Last intact company of 2nd US Infantry Regiment (Captain Patrick Phelon)

G Men from disintegrated units and civilians fighting in small groups or individually.

H Company of the Maryland Battalion (Captain Henry Carberry)

I Company of the Maryland Battalion (Captain William Buchanan)

J Men from disintegrated units and civilians fighting in small groups or individually.

K Volunteers intermittently operating 3 x 3-pdr guns.

L Men from disintegrated units and civilians fighting in small groups or individually

AFTERMATH

"The fortunes of this day," Sargent wrote after reaching Fort Jefferson, "will blacken a full page in the future annals of America." And so for a time it seemed. Soon Americans from New Hampshire to Georgia were singing *Sinclair's Defeat*, which would become one of the most popular songs in early 19th-century America.

For Washington, St Clair's report recalled bitter memories. At Monongahela he had commanded the retreating British army's rearguard. "Here," he shouted at his secretary, Tobias Lear, "Yes, here on this very spot I took leave of him... I said 'I will add but one word – beware of surprise.'" Washington soon regained his composure. "General St Clair," he said, "shall have justice... I will receive him without displeasure. I shall hear him without prejudice."

In the first congressional investigation in American history, Congress appointed a committee to determine the causes of the catastrophe. On November 4, 1791, St Clair should have been in a fort at Kekionga, awaiting with a garrison of 1,200 US Army regulars the onset of winter. More than 3,000 levies and militiamen, who had accompanied him on his advance, should have long since returned to their homes. He instead had been on a field 44 miles from Kekionga, unsure of his location, unaware of the Indians' capacities or intentions, with an army of 1,700 starving, freezing, and mostly untrained men.

The committee's report exonerated St Clair. The campaign's success had depended upon a complex recruiting and logistical operation. The Americans had grossly underestimated its difficulty. For a campaign to commence at remote Fort Washington, they had allowed less than four months to assemble 4,000 officers and men who had not yet been recruited, and vast quantities of supplies that had not yet even been ordered.

Testimony of the surviving officers addressed the cascading series of supply and training failures that followed the decision. If he had received "cartridge paper in proper time," St Clair told the committee, his soldiers would not have faced the enemy untrained. The axes available to build the trace and forts, Major David Ziegler testified, "when used would bend up like a dumpling." The tents, which provided no protection from rain or snow, were "truly infamous." Much of the gunpowder, ruined from storage in the tents, "would not carry a ball but a short distance." Ziegler, who had served as an officer in Prussian, Russian and American armies, told the committee that he "never saw such a degree of trouble thrown on the shoulders of any other general that I have served with, as upon General St Clair."

St Clair's ignorance of the area of operations added to the degree of trouble. Had he known that his road to Kekionga would be only 29 miles shorter than Harmar's trace, not 55, his campaign likely would have taken a different course. "We had no guides," he told the committee, "not a single person being found in the country who had ever been through it, and both the geography and topography were utterly unknown."

The committee paid less attention to the battle itself. Some criticized the American commander for not building breastworks to protect his soldiers. The Indians, St Clair responded, then would have besieged rather than attacked the camp. His army, which had little food, would have had to leave the breastworks and fight the battle that occurred.

St Clair attributed the battle's outcome to the low quality of his soldiers and overwhelming Indian numbers. Many of his soldiers, he said, "had never been in the woods in their lives." It was, he added, "probably the first time to many of them that they fired a gun." It also, he told the committee, "was physically impossible that an army posted as mine was, could be attacked in front and rear, and on both flanks, at the same instant, and that attack be kept up in every part for four hours without intermission, unless the enemy had been greatly superior in numbers."

The Americans, however, had not been outnumbered. They had fought on a field on which they were especially vulnerable to the tactics the Indians used. By compressing his camp into such a small area, St Clair allowed the Indians to surround his army, and exposed the men in his lines to fire from all directions. By concentrating his artillery in only two locations, he made it possible for the Indians to focus the fire that suppressed it. By dispersing almost 500 men in detached camps and outposts, he allowed the Indians to render more than a quarter of his army unable to assist effectively in the camp's defense. By failing to clear the surrounding woods, he dramatically diminished the ability of his army's firepower to inflict on the Indians the casualties that would have forced them to withdraw.

St Clair blamed Knox, Hodgdon, and the army's contractors for the supply and training failures that doomed his campaign. Many in Congress

LEFT
This Rufus F. Zogbaum engraving from Roosevelt's *St Clair's Defeat* shows the brief return of an American force to the battlefield on February 1, 1792. Sargent, who joined the expedition, wrote in his journal, "I was astonished to see the amazing effect of the enemy's fire… Every twig and bush seems to be cut down, and the saplings and trees marked with the utmost profusion of shot." (Photograph Courtesy of Harper's Magazine)

RIGHT
This portrait of Henry Knox by Constantino Brunidi is in the US Capitol. (Architect of the Capitol)

wanted to expand the committee proceedings into a broader investigation of the activities of Knox and the New York financier William Duer. Duer, a business partner of Knox and a friend of Alexander Hamilton, had aided in the financing of St Clair's campaign, and received in return the army's supply contract. In 1792 Duer's financial empire collapsed. Afraid that further investigation might end in a scandal that would destroy the new national government under the US Constitution, Congress proceeded no further.

St Clair continued to serve as Governor of the Northwest Territory until 1802, when he retired to his estate in western Pennsylvania. He later lost his land when those to whom he had loaned money failed to pay their debts. By 1812 he was living in a small log cabin, where he died in 1818. "Mine," he wrote in 1812, "was a laudable ambition, that of becoming the father of a country, and laying a foundation for the happiness of millions then unborn."

After the battle of the Wabash, Lieutenant-Colonel James Wilkinson assumed command of what remained of the US Army on the Ohio River frontier. As he acted to ensure that Fort Jefferson and Fort Hamilton could be held, militia forces assembled to protect the larger forts and stations. The emboldened Indians, however, raided deep into the areas of American settlement. In desperate engagements at settlers' cabins, American men, and often women and children, fought for their lives.

The response in Philadelphia proved the effectiveness of the new national government. As the Washington administration attempted to negotiate a peace treaty with the Indians it acted to create a force that could defeat them if negotiations failed. Congress appropriated funds for a new US Army, and enacted legislation that standardized the organization, equipment, and training of militia forces to conform with those of the US Army. Washington appointed Major-General Anthony Wayne as the US Army's new leader, who was one of the most celebrated commanders of the Revolutionary War. The actions reassured the western settlers. Despite the Indian attacks, few on the frontier, even in the Northwest Territory, abandoned their settlements. In 1792, Kentucky followed Vermont into the union, as the 15th state.

Wayne then succeeded where St Clair had failed. Prolonged negotiations allowed him time to train his soldiers and to obtain the supplies needed for an effective campaign. The defection of William Wells, who led an effective corps of American scouts, allowed Wayne to advance with information on the area of operations and enemy as accurate as that available to Indian commanders.

In 1793, Wayne built a new headquarters for the US Army at the site of St Clair's 13th Camp, named Fort Greeneville. On December 25, 1793, the Americans began building at the site of the battle itself a symbol of national resolve, which Wayne named Fort Recovery. On June 30 and July 1, 1794, 2,000 Indians and British militiamen attacked, but failed to take, the exposed American outpost.

On August 20, 1794, the Americans had their revenge for the battle of the Wabash. At Fallen Timbers they routed an army of Indians and British militiamen. Wayne then constructed at Kekionga the fort that St Clair had failed to build, which would give Fort Wayne, Indiana, its name.

In 1795, the Indians surrendered in the Treaty of Greeneville all of what is now Ohio south of a line through Fort Recovery. In 1796 the British evacuated Detroit. In 1803 a part of the Northwest Territory entered the union as Ohio, the 17th state.

The Indian commanders who had defeated St Clair all opposed any further war with the Americans. Some younger leaders, however, disagreed. In 1805 thousands of Ohio Indians embraced a new religion revealed in visions of the Prophet (Tenskwatawa). He and his brother, Tecumseh, established Prophetstown, an Indian village larger than Kekionga, near the site of St Clair's 13th Camp. In a campaign of witchcraft accusations, the Prophet's followers attacked and killed many older Indian leaders.

In 1808 hostility by Americans and many Ohio Indians forced the Prophet and his followers to move to a new Prophetstown in Indiana. There, in 1811, they attacked an American army led by William Henry Harrison. The Americans, however, prevailed at the battle of Tippecanoe.

The War of 1812 followed. In 1813, a British army, and more than 2,000 Indians led by Tecumseh and the Wyandot chief Roundhead, invaded Ohio. An American army, led by Harrison, repelled them. American ships, commanded by Commodore Oliver Hazard Perry, destroyed a British fleet at the battle of Lake Erie.

An American army, which included hundreds of Ohio Wyandots and Shawnee led by Tarhe and Black Hoof, then invaded Ontario. On October 5, 1813, that army, commanded by Harrison, destroyed a British and Indian army at the battle of the Thames. There Tecumseh died, and war on the Ohio River frontier finally ended.

The Miami Jean Baptiste de Richardville (Piniwa), and the Wyandot William Walker, Sr., (Sehstahroh) were among the young warriors at the battle who would become important figures in their tribes' 19th-century histories. In 1790 Walker drew this sketch of the great Wyandot chief Tarhe. (Courtesy of the Wyandot County (Ohio) Historical Society)

THE BATTLEFIELD TODAY

The course of the campaign leads through sites from Cincinnati to Fort Recovery, Ohio. A monument on Ludlow Street, in downtown Cincinnati, commemorates Fort Washington. The Cincinnati Museum Center, at 1301 Western Avenue, has exhibits on the fort.

Ludlow's Station was in Cumminsville, where a monument at the intersection of Knowlton and Mad Anthony streets, marks the site.

Fort Hamilton was in Hamilton, at 1 South Monument Avenue. The Butler County Soldiers, Sailors and Pioneers Monument, a museum with exhibits on the fort, is at the site.

The battlefield as it looks today. (Author's collection)

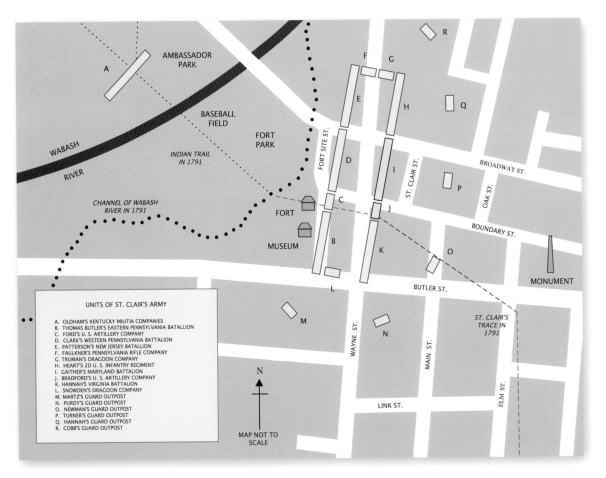

UNITS OF ST. CLAIR'S ARMY

A. OLDHAM'S KENTUCKY MILITIA COMPANIES
B. THOMAS BUTLER'S EASTERN PENNSYLVANIA BATALLION
C. FORD'S U. S. ARTILLERY COMPANY
D. CLARK'S WESTERN PENNSYLVANIA BATTALION
E. PATTERSON'S NEW JERSEY BATALLION
F. FAULKNER'S PENNSYLVANIA RIFLE COMPANY
G. TRUMAN'S DRAGOON COMPANY
H. HEART'S 2D U. S. INFANTRY REGIMENT
I. GAITHER'S MARYLAND BATTALION
J. BRADFORD'S U. S. ARTILLERY COMPANY
K. HANNAH'S VIRGINIA BATTALION
L. SNOWDEN'S DRAGOON COMPANY
M. MARTZ'S GUARD OUTPOST
N. PURDY'S GUARD OUTPOST
O. NEWMAN'S GUARD OUTPOST
P. TURNER'S GUARD OUTPOST
Q. HANNAH'S GUARD OUTPOST
R. COBB'S GUARD OUTPOST

MAP NOT TO SCALE

The 10th Camp, Camp Maple Swamp, was near Castine, where a marker on the west side of Ohio Route 127 commemorates the site.

Fort Jefferson was in the village of Fort Jefferson. The Fort Jefferson State Memorial, at the intersection of Ohio Route 121 and County Road 24, has markers explaining features of the fort.

The 13th Camp was in Greeneville. There the Garst Museum, at 205 N. Broadway, has extensive exhibits on St Clair's campaign.

The site of the 14th Camp, Camp Sulphur Springs, is marked by a monument on the west side of Ohio Route 49, 0.7 miles south of the Ohio Route 47.

The site of the 15th Camp, Camp Mississinewa, is marked by a monument on the east side of Ohio Route 49, where the road crosses the Mississinewa River.

The village of Fort Recovery now covers the battlefield. Visitors can easily find there the areas where events occurred during the battle. The Fort Recovery State Museum, at 1 Fort Site Street, has many artifacts recovered from the battlefield. The Fort Recovery Monument towers over the remains of the American dead.

BIBLIOGRAPHY

Anson, Bert, *The Miami Indians*, 1970

Bauman, R. F., "Pontiac's successor: the Ottawa Au-goosh-away," 26 *Northwest Ohio Quarterly*, Vol. 26, pp. 8–38, Bowling Green, Ohio, 1954

Carter, Harvey Lewis, *The Life and Times of Little Turtle: First Sagamore of the Wabash*, 1987

Denny, Ebenezer, *Military Journal of Major Ebenezer Denny*, 1859

DeRegnaucourt, Tony, *The Archaeology of Fort Recovery, Ohio: St Clair's Defeat, Nov. 4, 1791, and Wayne's Victory, June 30 and July 1, 1794*, 1996

Eid, Leroy V., "American Indian Military Leadership: St Clair's 1791 Defeat," *Journal of Military History*, Vol. 57, No. 1, pp. 71–88, Lexington, Virginia, 1993

Gaff, Alan D., *Bayonets in the Wilderness: Anthony Wayne's Legion in the Old Northwest*, 2004

Guthman, William H., *March to Massacre*, 1970

Hoffman, Phillip W., *Simon Girty: Turncoat Hero*, 2008

Jacobs, James R., *The Beginnings of the United States Army*, 1938

Katzenberger, George A,, "Major George Adams," *Ohio Archaeological and Historical Society Quarterly*, Vol. 22, pp. 522–42, Columbus, Ohio, 1913

Kohn, Richard H., *Eagle and Sword: The Federalists and the Creation of the Military Establishment in America, 1783–1802*, 1975

Littell, Stephen, "Memoir of Captain Eliakim Littell of Essex County, New Jersey," *Proceedings of the New Jersey Historical Society*, Vol. 7, pp. 83–104, Newark, New Jersey, 1882

Lytle, Richard M., *The Soldiers of America's First Army*, 2004

Mahon, John K., *American Militia: Decade of Decision, 1789–1800*, 1960

Meek, Basil, "Tarhe the Crane," *Ohio Archaeological and Historical Society Quarterly*, Vol. 20, pp. 64–73, Columbus, Ohio, 1911

Newman, Samuel, "A Picture of the First United States Army: the Journal of Captain Samuel Newman," *Wisconsin Magazine of History*, Vol. 2, No. 2, pp. 44–73, Madison, Wisconsin, 1918

Prucha, Francis P., *The Sword of the Republic: The United States Army on the Frontier, 1783–1846*, 1969

Roosevelt, Theodore, "St Clair's Defeat," *Harper's New Monthly Magazine*, Vol. 92, Issue 549, New York, 1896

Sargent, Winthrop, "Winthrop Sargent's Diary While with General Arthur St Clair's Expedition Against the Indians," *Ohio Archaeological and Historical Society Quarterly*, Vol. 33, pp. 237–73, Columbus, Ohio, 1924

Smith, Dwight L., "William Wells and the Indian Council of 1793," *Indiana Magazine of History*, Vol. 56, pp. 212–25, Indianapolis, Indiana, 1960

Smith, William Henry, *The St Clair Papers*, 1882

St Clair, Arthur, *A Narrative of the Campaign Against the Indians*, 1812

Steuben, Friedrich Wilhelm von, *Baron von Steuben's Revolutionary War Drill Manual: A Facsimile Reprint of 1794 Edition*, 1985

Sugden, John, *Blue Jacket*, 2000

Sword, Wiley, *President Washington's Indian War: the Struggle for the Old Northwest, 1790–1795*, 1985

Tanner, Helen H., *Atlas of Great Lakes Indian History*, 1986

Van Cleve, Benjamin, *Memoirs of Benjamin Van Cleve*, 1922

Van Trees, Robert, *Banks of the Wabash*, 2002

Weslager, Clinton A., *The Delaware Indians*, 1972

Wilson, Frazier, "St Clair's Defeat: As Told by an Eye-Witness," *Ohio Archaeological and Historical Society Quarterly*, Vol. 5, pp. 378–80, Columbus, Ohio. 1901

Wilson, Frazier, *Journal of Captain Daniel Bradley*, 1935